Evilyn Beecham

vj-94.

Lind Corley
Sheepscombe
15. viii. 2003

Limited edition, signed by
the Duchess of Kent

Music Enriches All

Her Royal Highness The Duchess of Kent, President of the College

Katharine

Music Enriches All

The Royal Northern College of Music
the First Twenty-One Years

MICHAEL KENNEDY

CARCANET

FOR KATHLEEN

First published in 1994 by
Carcanet Press Limited
208-212 Corn Exchange Buildings
Manchester M4 3BQ

Copyright © Michael Kennedy 1994

The right of Michael Kennedy to be identified
as the author of this work has been asserted by him in
accordance with the Copyright, Designs and Patents Act of 1988
All rights reserved

A CIP catalogue record for this book is
available from the British Library
ISBN 1 85754 085 9 (paperback)
ISBN 1 85754 111 1 (limited edition)

Design and production by Janet Allan
Set in 10/14 pt Sabon by Koinonia
Printed and bound in England by
Smith Settle, Otley

The Royal Northern College of Music wishes to acknowledge the support of the following pre-publication subscribers:

John Abendstern
David Adams
Freda J Adderley
Miss Susan Addison
Keith A Ahlquist
Ruth Aldred
Mary E Allan
Douglas W Allen
G C Allen
Fred and Reabie Alsberg
Lewis Anderson
Sir James Anderton
Keith Armes
Nicola Aronowitz
Robert Ashworth
Nora Askey
Associated Board of the Royal Schools of
    Music
Maureen and John Avery
Ryszard Bakst
Dagnija Balodis
Miss E Joan Bamford MBE LRAM
Phyllis M Bancroft
Enid Bandey (née Withers)
Mary I Clibran Barnes
Roderick J Barrand
Hilary Wish Barratt
Ignacio Amann Barroso
Philip J Bate
William E Baugh
Colin Bean MA
Pamela Beardmore-Nield ARNCM(P)
    ARNCM(T) LLCM(TD) ALCM
Charles Beare
Dr Gwilym Beechey
Dr Colin Beeson
P K Berry
John Bethell
Mrs Mildred Bettley
Jean M Binner
Dr J H L and Mrs S Birchall
Barbara F Birley
Dr Christopher A Birt
Edward Blakeman
Shirley Blakey
Rudolf Botta
Ian Charles Boulter

Dr Joyce Bourne
John W Bower
Paula Jane Bradbury LWCMD PGRNCM
Stephen Michael Bradshaw
Arthur E Brereton
Mary M Brewer (née Hodgson) ARMCM
Gerald A Brinnen
David J Brookes
Pamela R Brooks
Maurice and Jean Buckley
Anne Burford GRNCM
Mr N Burgess
Denise Burns
Sheila Burton
Rachel Sarah Butcher
John Byrne GRNCM
Teresa Cahill LRAM AGSM
George Caird
Jennifer Beth Caldwell
Dorothy Cambridge
John Cameron
N A Cameron
Vivienne Campbell
Douglas R Carrington
Colonel and Mrs G E Cauchi
Eric Chadwick
Ruth Charles
Brian E Chesworth
Irene M Christopherson
Edward A Clark
Tim Clark
Alice and Doug Clarke
Janice Close
Brenda B Clowes
Arnaldo Cohen
Kathleen Collins
David and Sheila Cook
Geoffrey Cooke
P J D Cooke
John T Coope
Ava-June Cooper MADAM
Mr and Mrs R H R Cooper
Heather Corbett
Robert and Sylvia Cornish
Sydney Coulston
David Cowdy
Charles W P Cracknell MBE ARAM

Joan A Crampton
Alan and Barbara Cross
Marjorie and Walter Dale
J H and N Daniels
Michael d'Arcy
Gwen C Davidge
Garedd O Davies
Professor Graham Dawber
Kenneth A Deighton MBE
Gita Denise AMA (Prague)
Miss Muriel Dicks
Mr and Mrs W B Dobie
Sylvia Dobney
Professor and Mrs C R Dodwell
Brian K Douglas
Pauline Dowse
Mrs Christine Drew (née Sutcliffe)
Martin J Drew
Jack Drinkall
Denis Drury
David Dugdale
Dr M and Mrs E M Dukes
Sharon Lynn Dunning
E Glyn Durden
David and Mavis Dyson
Graham Eccles
Philip L Edwards
John Egan
David Ellis
Jane English
Mr and Mrs Elwyn Evans
Alison A Ferrie
John Fewkes
Mrs W F Fincham
Rebecca Firth
Mr Alban Fisher
George Fisher
Margaret Olive Fitton
Sir Denis Forman
Mavis Fox
David Francis
Brenda Fraser
Professor Malcolm and Fay Fraser
Michael J Freegard FCIS HonRNCM
Jack Furse
Derek Gaggs
Rachel Gick

Rachel Pickering
Christopher Pigram
Dorothy Pilling
Thomas B Pitfield
Thomas Pitt
Miss Nicola J Plant
Mr P Plowman
Helen Powell
Derek and Gio Prendergast
John L Macdonald Price BA
Leila F H Priddle LGSM
Betty Proctor (née Quinn)
Sir Idwal Pugh KCB
Michael Purton
Andrew Rackham
Arthur Renshaw
Prof. Hans-Dieter Resch
Timothy Reynish
John Reynolds GRSM ARCM LRAM
Mr Stephen Charles Reynolds
Florence M Rhodes
Bethan Richards
David W Riley
William T Risby (Lord Mayor of Manchester)
Mary Roach
G H Roberts
Mavis Robinson
Maureen Sarah Roche
Martin Roscoe
John Rotherham
Christopher Rowland
Royal Academy of Music
Royal College of Music
Royal Scottish Academy of Music and Drama
Paul R Salter
Gerard Emile Samson-Dekker
Katherine R Samuels (née Davis)
Dr A A Savage
Neil and Gillian Sawyer
Jacqueline Ann Schlaefli
Professor John E Scott
Joyce E Scott
Lesley Scully
Carol Seddon
Geoffrey Kent Senior

Philip Shaw
Mrs Christine L Sheridan
Timothy P Slack
Rodney Slatford
Anna Smart
Clive F Smart
Adrienne Smith
Mrs Joyce Smith
John G Smithson
A W Snowise
Clare Stammeijer-Southworth
Jonathan C Starkey
Dr Jim Steeley
Robin H Stewart
Suzy Stonefield
M Pamela Stones
J G Storry
Sun Alliance Insurance UK Ltd – Broker
    Division
Ka Kit Tam
Allan E Taylor
Laurence Taylor
Malcolm and Beryl Taylor
Val and Dennis Taylor
Wilfred and Jennifer Theakstone
Katey Thomas
Hutch Thomson
Stephen Threlfall
Colonel John B Timmins OBE TD DSc
Christine Elizabeth Tomlinson
Professor John Tomlinson CBE
Marion Tootell
Sir Simon Towneley KCVO
Helen Trueman
D E Tucker
John and Margaret Turner
Christopher Underwood
Susan Valentine
Eduardo Vassallo
Air Commodore M C M Vaughan CBE
    RAF (Retd)
Ursula Vaughan Williams
Dr P A Vice
Mrs M Vitti
Lillian Wain (née Brocklehurst)

Stephen John Walker
Rosemary Jean Walton BMus ARMCM
Eleanor Warren MBE FRNCM FGSM
David W Watson
Alison Weatherburn
N W Webster
Brian C Wedgbury
Percy Welton
Jean White
Mrs G E Whitehead
Richard Whitehouse
J P V Whittaker MA(Oxon)
Mrs V Whittaker
Malcolm C Whittell
Miss Irené P Wilde
J T Wilkinson
Marion Wilkinson
Nigel P Wilkinson
Sir David Willcocks
Graham and Pam Williams
Vanessa Williamson
Ann, Ron and Jane Willis
D Wilmot
Wilmslow Hotel
Catherine Wilson
Mr D G Wilson OBE DL
John Wilson
Trevor Wilson
Herbert Winterbottom DMus
    MSc FNSM FTCL LRAM
J B Wishart-Hodgson
Jean Wolstenholme
Maimie Woods
Joseph Woolwich
David J Woonton
Ian Wright
Jocelyn Wright
Arthur Wroe
Trevor Wye FRNCM
Christopher Yates
Vera Yates
Alexander Young FRNCM
Dr David Young
Yossi Zivoni

Contents

Preface

At 21, the Royal Northern College of Music is, as we say in Lancashire, 'nobbut a lad' and therefore this is scarcely the time to attempt an historical analysis of its role. But in a very short time it has accumulated a formidable list of achievements and an international reputation to go with it. Building on the foundation laid over many years by its two constituent founding colleges, it rapidly went from strength to strength. This book, therefore, is inevitably a chronicle of events rather than an 'in-depth' study; and if there are a lot of names and if the content of the chapters follows the pattern of the years, I can only plead for the reader's patience and say that these are people and events deserving of record.

Inevitably, because space is limited if expense is not to become prohibitive, many events are not mentioned. The concerts and recitals given at the College since 1973 would fill a book by themselves. I have tried to be selective and to give a flavour of the music-making. A college like the Royal Northern is the sum of very many individual parts and each part is crucial. I would have liked to mention everybody, but that was clearly impossible and I can only apologise to those who are omitted and ask for their forbearance.

In writing the book I have had unstinted help from many people, particularly, of course, the Principal, Sir John Manduell. I express my special gratitude to him and to Dr Colin Beeson and Mr Christopher Yates, to Dame Kathleen Ollerenshaw and Sir Simon Towneley, and to Ms Marian Blaikley, the College's Press Officer, who has tirelessly and patiently provided me with material, press cuttings and encouragement and has assembled the illustrations. I am indebted to Miss Ida Carroll and Mr Robert Elliott for their documentation of the early days of the College and the events leading up to its establishment and to Dr Beeson and his secretary, Mrs Carol Booth, for compiling the Appendices. I also thank Mr John Rawnsley for lending me some photographs and giving me valuable information, and Miss Sian Edwards, Miss Joan Rodgers, Mr Patrick McGuigan, Mr Christopher Rowland, and Mr Peter Donohoe for their reminiscences. I also thank Mr Thomas B. Pitfield for allowing me to quote his poem on the foundation-stone-laying of the College. My thanks, too, to Dr Joyce Bourne for typing my by no means immaculate manuscript.

Clearly, everyone connected with the College could tell their own story.

Although I have been proud to serve on its governing bodies from the start, I have also spent hours in the place as a professional critic divorcing myself from a natural pride in its achievements in order to arrive, I hope, at reasonably objective judgments. This book is my view of the College and I alone am responsible for its errors and omissions. I hope what I have written here will be useful to the historian of the first fifty years. I offer it as my tribute to an establishment which may not be beautiful from the outside, but has a warm heart and a welcoming smile for all who enter it, whether as student, staff, or listener.

M.K.

SELECT BIBLIOGRAPHY

Kennedy, Michael: *The History of the Royal Manchester College of Music, 1893-1972* (Manchester University Press, 1972).

Robert-Blunn, John: *Northern Accent: the Life Story of the Northern School of Music* (John Sherratt & Son, Altrincham, 1972).

Thomason, Geoffrey: *The Royal Manchester College of Music, 1893-1973* (RNCM, 1993).

I Pre-History

Twenty-one years have passed since the Royal Northern College of Music in Manchester was officially opened, yet already one wonders how the city's musical life managed without it. Any account of its history, however brief, must go back much further, to 15 November 1954 when the Council of the Royal Manchester College of Music authorised the Principal, Frederic R. Cox, to explore amalgamation with the Northern School of Music. It was thought that where financial support was concerned, one institution might fare better than two. So began a process which was to take nearly 18 arduous years to come to fruition. Both institutions flourished in buildings which were totally inadequate in size and design. The RMCM had been founded in 1893 with Sir Charles Hallé as Principal. Since 1854 he had been urging the need for a conservatoire in Manchester so that local talent could be trained properly. A building in Ducie Street, off Oxford Road, built but never used as a club, was purchased and presented to the college, which admitted its first students on 2 October 1893. Among them was a baritone from Oldham, Charles Walton, who nine years later was to have a son William. The boy became Sir William Walton OM, the composer. Hallé died in October 1895 and was succeeded by the great Russian violinist Adolph Brodsky, who had come to Manchester only a month earlier as professor of violin. He was only one of several illustrious international figures who taught at the college, among them the pianists Wilhelm Backhaus and Egon Petri, the violinists Arthur Catterall and Henry Holst, and the singers Norman Allin and Marie Brema. Brodsky was Principal until his death in 1929 and was succeeded by R.J. Forbes (1929-53).

Among the outstanding inter-war students were the composer Alan Rawsthorne, the violinist Raymond Cohen and the pianist Gordon Green who became a teacher of remarkable quality both at the RMCM and the Royal Northern College of Music. When Cox, an outstanding singing teacher, took over in 1953, the college's opera performances attained new distinction and national fame when students such as Elizabeth Harwood, Rosalind Plowright, Ann Murray, Anne Howells, Joseph Ward, Ryland Davies and John Mitchinson took part. In the mid-1950s there arose a remarkable group of *avant-garde* composers – Alexander Goehr, Peter Maxwell Davies, Harrison Birtwistle and John Ogdon, also a virtuoso pianist – who were either pupils of or influenced by Richard Hall, professor of harmony and counterpoint. They were known as the New Manchester Group.

The Northern School of Music had existed since 1920. It began as the Manchester branch of the Matthay School of Music and moved out of the centre of the city to premises in Oxford Road in 1934. After 23 years as a private concern, it 'went public' in 1943 and was incorporated as the Northern School of Music. In 1952 the Burnham Committee approved graduate status for students 'who fulfil the special conditions established by the School'. Although the School concentrated for many years on teacher-training, under Ida Carroll's guidance more stress began to be laid on performance. Among those who befriended the School were the pianist Clifford Curzon and the conductor Charles Groves. Its teaching staff included the instrumentalists Maurice Clare, Reginald Stead, John Wilson, Irene Wilde, and Eileen Chadwick, and the singers Ellis Keeler and Albert Haskayne. Its first opera (*The Bartered Bride*) was staged in July 1952. Thereafter there were an annual opera and several splendid choral concerts conducted by, among others, Maurice Handford, who was Sir John Barbirolli's associate conductor with the Hallé from 1966. The School produced many distinguished instrumentalists and singers, among them the violinist Colin Staveley, the sopranos Pauline Tinsley and Alison Hargan, the contralto Alfreda Hodgson, and the bass Ian Comboy.

In 1955, the Northern School's founder and Principal, Hilda Collens, met Cox and friendly, informal talks were held. But she died in April 1956 when the proposed amalgamation had already 'gone cold', several members of the NSM Council believing that the two institutions differed too widely in character and method for any merger to be satisfactory. The RMCM meanwhile had decided that perhaps its future lay in a strengthening of existing ties with the University of Manchester. The new NSM Principal, Ida Carroll, also met Cox but, while seeing the force of the argument for amalgamation, did not favour the idea. The NSM, though, was in financial need and sought a higher grant from Manchester Education Committee. The committee's chairman, Alderman Abraham Moss, agreed to assist the NSM substantially but was also toying with the idea of a new municipal school of music involving both existing establishments. The RMCM was opposed to this idea. The NSM decided to forget the RMCM and to throw in its lot with the education committee and there the merger idea might have foundered for ever had not a new factor come into the equation.

In July 1958 Percy Lord, education officer for Lancashire County Council, sounded out both the RMCM and the NSM about the possibility of talks on music education in Lancashire. On 10 December a meeting of local authorities – Lancashire and Cheshire County Councils, Manchester City Council and Salford City Council – and the two colleges was held at the NSM at which, for the first time, mention of a complete new music conservatoire was made. A draft scheme existed by April 1959. This acknowledged that there were difficulties regarding the RMCM's Royal Charter and Treasury grant, but was optimistic and agreed that the new institution should be in Manchester. By June 1960 names for the new college were being discussed. The NSM supported Royal Northern Academy of Music. By September this had been changed to Royal Northern College of Music, Manchester, although Cox favoured Royal School of Music, Manchester. It was nevertheless pointed out that permission for the prefix Royal lay in the Queen's prerogative and could not be sought until the establishment existed.

Sir Simon Towneley, one of the RNCM's earliest champions, at the Congregation of Awards 1990 when he was awarded the College's highest honour and became a Companion. Photograph: Camera Five Four

The NSM attitude at this stage was that it was willing to cooperate in a scheme for the new college by the local authorities but was unwilling to amalgamate with the RMCM as a voluntary college or as a voluntary college maintained by local authorities. Its Council stated: 'Although its financial assets are negligible, the NSM has a goodwill established by 40 years of hard labour and this is an asset which should be considered of equal importance to the work of the RMCM where substantial grants have been received.' Reading between the lines, it is clear how deep the divisions between the two colleges went.

On 24 January 1961 the recently formed steering committee for the new college decided that it should be fully maintained by local authority funds and that the RMCM's Royal Charter would have to go. Lancashire would provide the clerk of an interim governing body and Manchester the treasurer. On the steering committee, of which the chairman was Alderman Mrs Fletcher of Lancashire County Council, was Simon Towneley, a member since 1961 of the County Council and an authority on Venetian opera, which he had studied with Egon Wellesz. He had noticed a minute about the negotiations for a new college and had been sent a paper about the subject on which he had commented 'More counterpoint than harmony'. After Mrs Fletcher's death, Towneley took over the chairmanship but, after one meeting, lost his seat on the County Council. He was succeeded by Alderman Sir Maurice Pariser of Manchester City Council. The committee met in Manchester Town Hall. The decision to go ahead with the establishment of the new college was taken in May 1961. At its first meeting, on 21 November 1962, the interim governing body decided that a Joint Committee should be formed as soon as possible. A site on the corner of Oxford Road and Booth Street West occupying 315ft by 190ft was earmarked for the college, which

The College in the final stages of completion.
Photograph: Elsam, Mann & Cooper

was to go into the 1964-5 building programme. Four months later Bickerdike, Allen, Rich and Partners of London were appointed as architects. This was not achieved without difficulty. Towneley consulted his friend Edward Boyle, then Minister of Education. Manchester City Council and Lancashire County Council had opposing views on the choice of architect; the Ministry of Education (as it still was) strongly advocated the Bickerdike firm and made it obvious that its goodwill depended on this choice. Towneley was impressed by W.H. Allen, an expert on acoustics, when he invited him to dinner at the Turf Club, an unlikely setting for a musical discussion – its walls were more accustomed to talk, by the old Tory grandees, on the great issues of the day. But Allen's partner Bickerdike took charge. He proved to be a difficult man with whom to deal. Towneley remembers the look on the face of the Austrian organ-builder Hradetsky when he was shown Bickerdike's stark white design for the College organ-case – not a curve, not an angel, nothing baroque in sight. Geraint Jones, the College's organ consultant, always referred to Bickerdike, to his fury, as the *Gauleiter* or 'Herr Bicker-dickie'.

The Joint Committee of 31 members was formally established in 1966. It first met in Manchester Town Hall on 27 October of that year. Its composition represented the four authorities, four members each from the colleges, delegates from other organisations, and Sir Percy Lord, as he now was, as foundation member. Simon Towneley, who was elected to the Councils of the NSM in 1966 and of the RMCM in 1967, was co-opted to the staffing and architectural sub-committees. The first chairman was Alderman Sir Maurice Pariser. He died on 3 February 1968 and was succeeded by Alderman Mrs Kathleen Ollerenshaw.

To detail the bureaucratic delays and inquiries of the next five years and to recount the many meetings about what would happen to each college's assets, funds, pension funds, scholarships, etc, would weary the reader, not to mention the writer. In addition, the nation as a whole went through its periodic economic crisis. When the college was taken out of the 1968 building programme because 'it would be inappropriate at this juncture to commit £³/₄ million on a single monotechnic project, however worthy', Jack Boyce, who had succeeded Lord as Lancashire's chief education officer, and was one of the founding fathers to whom the College owes most, wrote: 'A dreadful blow. There can have been very few projects which met so many obstacles.'

In September 1968 the Department of Education and Science approved the college's inclusion in the 1969-70 building programme at an estimated cost of £880,360 (gross), work to start as soon as possible after 1 April 1969. A tender from H. Fairweather & Co Ltd to build the college for £828,299 was accepted on 27 June 1969, a start to be made on 10 November and the building to be completed within 27 months. The college was to include an opera theatre seating 628, concert hall (capacity 500), recital room seating up to 250, lecture theatre, library, nearly 100 teaching and practice rooms, refectory, common rooms, kitchens, and administrative offices. The number of students was agreed initially at 450 (300 RMCM, 150 NSM). It had always been tacitly assumed that the college's Principal would be a 'neutral' choice and that neither of the existing Principals would be appointed. In any case, Cox resigned as Principal of the RMCM in September 1970 (he became Principal Emeritus) and Dr John Wray was appointed Acting Principal. The new college post was advertised in June 1969 – and re-advertised a year later. It was offered in September 1970 to John Manduell, director of music at Lancaster University since 1968 and before that chief planner of the BBC Music Programme from 1964. He was 42 and was also a composer. Born in Johannesburg, Manduell went to London to study at the Royal Academy of Music where he was Performing Right Society scholar in composition. His teacher was Lennox Berkeley. After two years as conductor and broadcaster in South Africa, he joined the BBC music staff in London in 1956. He was appointed BBC Head of Music for the Midlands and East Anglia until returning to London in 1964 when the BBC Music Programme (one of the earlier forms of Radio 3) was inaugurated.

Manduell's name was first put forward – again at the Turf Club, at a meeting with Kathleen Ollerenshaw, Simon Towneley and John Cruft, music adviser to the Arts Council – by Charles Groves, at that time conductor of the Royal Liverpool Philharmonic Orchestra and a member of the Council of the NSM since 1950. Some Manchester councillors then urged a candidate with 'local authority experience', but the majority voted for Manduell. He was released from his Lancaster post through the magnanimity of Charles Carter, Vice-Chancellor of Lancaster University, who had persuaded the university to invest a large sum of money in the music department, including a new building, and was convinced that he had found the right man to establish it. Towneley wrote privately to Carter to warn him of what was afoot. He sent a charming reply but added in his own hand 'Damn you!'. When Manduell appeared before the selection committee, chaired by Kathleen Ollerenshaw, all agreed that he was the man. The Chairman read out his references. William Glock, then BBC Controller of Music, was ambivalent and scarcely encouraging. When reproached about this by Towneley some time later, he was amazed. 'After that,' Towneley said, 'I felt I

The Concert Hall during construction.

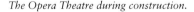

The Opera Theatre during construction.

Dame Kathleen Ollerenshaw, Chairman of the Joint Committee. Photograph: Ian Coates Photography

understood the way a BBC mind works.' Manduell accepted the college post as from 1 September 1971. In the meantime he acted as an adviser to the Joint Committee. He also visited conservatoires in the United States, Western and Eastern Europe and the Soviet Union to study and compare teaching methods and curricula.

A potential threat to the start on building the college came from the possibility that the site could be 'occupied' by gipsies. They had been camping on land in Rusholme and one of their tactics was to move on to a site where building was about to begin. The law was vague enough to make the police reluctant to move them by force, particularly if a site had been 'marked off' so that it was no longer public land. Some gipsies had recently been evicted from sites earmarked for extensions to Manchester Royal Infirmary and the college site was a tempting next port of call. If it were to be occupied, obtaining a court order against the gipsies would be a lengthy process and could mean that the college would lose its place in the building programme yet again.

The bulldozers were due to move on to the site on a Monday morning. The chairman of the Joint Committee, Dame Kathleen Ollerenshaw (as she now was), drove there in her white Rover from her Didsbury home several times during the day on the Sunday. Convinced that there was a real risk of occupation, she drove round and round the site through the night. At 8.30 am the work began.

Radical savings on the lowest tender were now found to be needed. The briefing for the building was altered so often that it was only through the patience of the architects that it was completed. Major economies were made on the foundations, the heating and ventilation and in changes to the general structure and internal walls. The architects put forward the idea, on advice from heating engineers, that the estimates on the boilers could be halved. This led later to immense problems and great additional expense (it was soon found that half the tutorial rooms lacked any form of heating and £26,000 was spent at once on remedial work. More followed). Why was it allowed? It could cynically be said that no one argues with the experts when their advice provides what is required: a dramatic decrease in estimated costs and, consequently, success in getting into the building programme.

Even so, by 1971-2 the estimated total cost of the college had risen to £1,371,050 and this was to prove optimistic. On 1 April 1971, the foundation stone was laid jointly by Frederic Cox and Ida Carroll, whose kiss at the ceremony had all the warmth that might be expected if Edward Heath were to kiss Margaret Thatcher. But at least things were now happening. The building was going up and an Association of Friends of the new college was formed, with Simon Towneley as chairman and Ida Carroll as honorary secretary. Towneley had played a major part in all the negotiations for the new college and was to a large degree responsible for Lancashire's generous enthusiasm for and support of the project. It was also decided that there should be, from the start, an organ in the concert hall. Controversially, and with Geraint Jones as adviser, a contract was arranged with the firm of George Hradetsky of Krems, Austria, because 'tracker action' was required and there was difficulty about obtaining this from a British organ-builder. The cost of the instrument was £40,000. Only £20,000 was allocated in the estimate; the remaining half was raised by a donation of £4,000 from the Association of Friends and £16,000 from various trusts and private individuals.

Ida Carroll speaking at the foundation-stone ceremony. On her left is Dame Kathleen Ollerenshaw. On Miss Carroll's right is Frederic Cox, and on his right stands John Bickerdike, the new College's architect.

Admission of students for 1972-3 was to be to the new college, then officially known as the Northern College of Music. Administrative 'fusion' of the RMCM, the NSM and the new college was fixed for 31 July 1972 and the new governing body took over the College on 1 September 1972. The Joint Committee's complement was a chairman (Dame Kathleen Ollerenshaw), vice-chairman, 16 local government representatives (six from Lancashire, four from Cheshire County Council, four from Manchester City Council and two from Salford City Council), four life-members from the RMCM and four from the NSM, and one representative apiece from Manchester University, the Arts Council, the BBC, Granada TV, the Hallé Concerts Society and the Royal Liverpool Philharmonic Society. Manduell had meanwhile been busy with the steering committee making plans for the curriculum and, in July 1972, proposing the creation of a junior division such as had existed in both the constituent establishments. There was also much debate about the first opera to be presented by the new college in the Opera Theatre in December 1972. Manduell proposed a scheme of four operas during the first year (one in the Michaelmas term, two in the Lent term and one in the summer). He suggested that Walton's *Troilus and Cressida*, as an appropriate choice by a Lancashire-born composer, should be the first production, with a former NSM student, Alison Hargan, as Cressida, Joseph Ward (ex-RMCM) as Troilus, and John Rawnsley (NSM – RNCM) as Diomede. By April 1972 this was found to be out of the question and the committee reverted to its first idea of a triple bill comprising Walton's one-act comic opera *The Bear*, Gordon Crosse's *Purgatory* (a setting of W.B. Yeats's one-act play), and a choral work to be commissioned from John McCabe or, failing him, John Gardner or Peter Maxwell Davies. In the event, no new work materialised and the third part

Vyna Martin and John Rawnsley in Walton's The Bear, 1973. Photograph courtesy John Rawnsley

of the bill, performed in February 1973, was Walton's *Belshazzar's Feast*. Manduell had originally invited Alan Rawsthorne to write either a one-act or full-length opera to open the theatre, but the composer died in July 1971 before the idea had any chance to develop.

Despite a national building strike in August 1972, the College was available for partial use from 18 September. The 'old' colleges were used for overflow tuition. This tended to prolong old rivalries and tempers already frayed became severely tattered. But it was the right decision. Teaching in the new building began 'officially' on 8 January 1973. Much committee time had already been spent on discussion of the amount to be spent on equipping the new college. Forty-eight new Steinway pianos were required, but Manchester Corporation's finance committee would agree to pay only for 24. There was a lively chauvinistic controversy about the relative merits of Steinways and British-made pianos, just as there had been about British and Austrian organs. 'A damned disgrace', said a British manufacturer and Simon Towneley, presenting the treasurer's report at the RMCM annual general meeting, rebuked Manchester City Council for 'holding up orders for vital equipment which could delay the opening of the college'. Towneley feared that Manchester's attitude to the new college was in danger of becoming smugly 'provincial' in the worst sense of the word. The fracas served notice on the College that it would need to fight to attain the ideal proclaimed by John Manduell, writing for the College's first brochure on the day he assumed his post (1 September 1971), when he said that 'our hope, and indeed intention, must be to make the new College an exciting and significant place, a place where it is a privilege to work, a place where the highest standards are sought after, a place where the only ultimate criterion is quality'. For this privilege each of the first intake of students was required to pay £75.00 a year. (In 1994 European Community students must pay £2,770, the rest £6,000).

An important item of expenditure over which there was less controversy was the purchase of a students' hall of residence. It became known during 1972 (through the enterprise of Ida Carroll and John Manduell, helped by W.P. Lockley, a member of the NSM Council) that the Methodist theological college in Alexandra Road South, known as Hartley Victoria College, was for sale for the remarkably low figure of £304,000. It had six acres of grounds and today accommodates over 170 students in centrally heated rooms. The four local authorities on the Joint Committee approved the purchase price during 1973, plus a five-year first phase of repairs and renovations at £115,000 (later inevitably increased) and furnishings to the value of £21,000. Formal purchase was

Cricket at Hartley Hall.

completed on 6 June 1974. New kitchens were installed and, in addition to individual study rooms, Hartley Hall, as it was renamed, had its own recital room. The grounds contain a football field, tennis court, croquet lawn and gardens. It was officially opened by the Duchess of Kent on 7 December 1976, but the first College Christmas dinner was held there two years earlier, with the first College carol service in its chapel. Dr Percy Scott was appointed as its first Warden and he was succeeded by David Andrews in March 1977. The RNCM thus became unique among British music colleges in owning suitable and convenient accommodation for the benefit of students.

But no one, not even perhaps its designer, would claim that the new college itself was a building notable for architectural beauty. 'Functional' was one description, 'Colditz' another. Its concrete exterior has the period look of the 1960s. Nor can it be overlooked that internally it left much to be desired. There was no lift for the benefit of those whose health was not improved by climbing stairs. The teething-troubles required dentistry on a mammoth scale. The problems of heating and ventilation continued for years and the secretarial and other staff on the top floor worked in primitive conditions where heat and light were concerned. But a key to the success of the College from the start was the open aspect of its ground floor – the Concourse, refectory and halls. Where in many colleges one is met by a reception desk and a labyrinth of corridors, here

John Manduell with Col. Robert and Dame Kathleen Ollerenshaw with John Manduell at the opening of the roof garden in memory of their daughter Florence, 26 June 1974.

The Duchess of Kent with Dame Kathleen Ollerenshaw, followed by the Principal, visit the roof garden during the official opening of the College on 28 June 1973.

one was admitted at once into the life of the place. From the start, too, it had a delightful feature invisible from the street. This is the roof garden donated by Colonel Robert and Dame Kathleen Ollerenshaw in memory of their daughter Florence, who died aged 26 in 1972. They opened it officially on 26 June 1974. In 1975 they added a water sculpture designed, like the garden, by Michael Brown. Thus the College had an oasis of nature and beauty in a desert of brick and concrete.

The College was officially opened nine months after it had first come into use. The Duchess of Kent performed the ceremony at 11.30am on 28 June 1973, a day of sunshine and strong breeze, when the guests had a lunch of melon, roast beef, and strawberries and cream. Again there was controversy, this time over the spending of £2,600 on a rest-room and lavatory for the Duchess. This was partly responsible for the cost of the opening exceeding the estimate nearly fivefold. The new college, its critics felt, believed too wholeheartedly in extravagance. But an announcement dated 17 July stated: 'The Queen has been graciously pleased to command that the title "Royal" be included in the name of the Northern College of Music, Manchester, in perpetuation of the title enjoyed by the Royal Manchester College of Music with which the Northern School of Music has amalgamated to form the new College.' This had come about principally through the interest of Sir Philip Woodfield, then Assistant Under-Secretary of State at the Home Office. Ida Carroll had been against a Royal prefix, but Cox wanted one, having agreed to give up the Royal Charter. Simon Towneley had several Turf Club meetings with Woodfield on the subject. Sir Philip suggested that 'Royal' could be perpetuated in a title without conferring any special status, as in Theatre Royal or Royal Exchange. On this basis he steered the matter through a byzantine process.

On the same day that the 'Royal' title was bestowed, the College was formally adopted as a member of the Associated Board of the Royal Schools of Music. In October the Queen consented to become Patron of the RNCM and the Duchess of Kent accepted the Presidency. It was the end of the beginning.

II Foundations

John Manduell's strategy was clear from the outset. He was Principal of an entirely new college. The fact that it was an amalgamation of two former institutions would cease to be relevant within a few years when the last students admitted to the RMCM and NSM gained their diplomas and would thereafter merely be an historic fact. As Thomas Pitfield, professor of harmony and counterpoint in the RMCM and for the first year of the RNCM, wrote at the time of the laying of the foundation stone:

> Two die, and one is born,
> Hail and farewell;
> Let mourning organ swell
> And heralding trumpets play:
> The best Tomorrow has its roots
> In Yesterday.

Manduell's task, therefore, was to insist at every point that the RNCM policy and procedures were what counted while at the same time realising that there would inevitably be frictions between staff and students from the two 'rival' establishments who now had to accustom themselves to being part of a new unity. 'I shall not enjoy it much for the first two years, but after that it will be all right,' he told a *Guardian* interviewer. But some survivors from that time maintain that what tension existed was between students from the old colleges and the first RNCM intake rather than between the staffs who, on the whole, co-operated well from the start. There was a suspicion that both colleges had lowered standards for their final intake. Diplomacy and Machiavellian skills learned in the labyrinthine power politics of the BBC now proved their worth for Manduell; and to his lasting credit he consistently rose and rode above the unavoidable pettinesses of human behaviour, while understanding them, to imprint an RNCM hallmark on everything the new college did. And if some of the older staff members looked askance or with suspicion at the apparently vaulting, sky's-the-limit ambition of their young Principal, disapproved of his commitment to contemporary music, and even found him 'remote' at first, they soon came to admire and respect his energy, skill in negotiation and tireless dedication to his job, his staff and his students. The students found him

Air Commodore Mansel Vaughan, the College's first Secretary.

Alexander Young, the first Head of Vocal Studies.

Left to right: Terence Greaves, Ida Carroll and Dr John Wray.

The first two Heads of Keyboard Studies: Clifton Helliwell (left) and his successor Robert Elliott.

approachable and appreciated that he treated them as adults and young professionals. John Rawnsley, now a leading baritone, told me of the contrast he encountered in the atmosphere and attitudes at the RNCM. At the Northern School of Music, even though he was over 21 when he started there, he had felt like a schoolboy under scrutiny (as had some of the staff). There were other students, however, who were not sure if their approachable Principal would have recognised them if he had passed them in the street.

Because of the long period of uncertainty before the new College was established, teachers in the old colleges were worried about their future and there were some resignations. 'I defy anyone to say I could have done more,' Manduell said. 'You cannot, and I will not, arouse expectations which might not be fulfilled. That is irresponsible and would not be wanted by anyone.' His first task was to make his own appointments. The first Secretary was Air Commodore Mansel Vaughan, who brought Service efficiency and personal charm to the administration of the College. Terence Greaves was appointed Dean of Development and the two former colleges' Principals, Ida Carroll and John Wray, became Dean of Management and Dean of Studies respectively. In September 1973 six schools of study were established: Composition and Performance, with Manduell and Greaves as heads of department; Keyboard Studies, headed by Clifton Helliwell; Strings (Cecil Aronowitz); Theory and Humanities (Wray); Wind and Percussion (no head at first); and Vocal Studies (Alexander Young). Some celebrated names were already on the staff, with tutors from the old colleges blended with a new intake. In the Composition School, tutors included Peter Maxwell Davies, Anthony Gilbert, and Thomas Pitfield. An array of keyboard tutors included Ryszard Bakst, Marjorie Clementi, Robert Elliott (harpsichord), Gordon Green, George Hadjinikos, Colin Horsley, Hedwig Stein, Kendall Taylor, John Wilson, Herbert Winterbottom (organ) and Derrick Wyndham.

Among the string teachers were Adrian Beers, Rudolf Botta, Maurice Clare, Sydney Errington, Clifford Knowles, Ludmila Navratil, Frederick Riddle, Bernard Shore, Raphael Sommer, Terence Weil and Yossi Zivoni. The theorists included John Bertalot, Keith Bond, Derrick Cantrell, Paul Crunden-White, Robert Elliott, Ronald Frost, Geoffrey Jackson, Hélène Pax, Dorothy Pilling, Nicholas Smith and Percy Welton. For wind and percussion the College could call on (to name only a few) Sydney Coulston (horn), Charles Cracknell (bassoon), Sidney Fell (clarinet), Jack Gledhill (timpani), Peter Graeme (oboe), Philip Jones (trumpet), Patricia Morris (flute), Terence Nagle (trombone), Bernard

O'Keefe (oboe), Fritz Spiegl (recorder), and William Waterhouse (bassoon). Alexander Young's singing school at first numbered 18 tutors, including Frederic Cox, Caroline Crawshaw, Albert Haskayne, Sylvia Jacobs, Leslie Langford (widow of the great music critic of the *Manchester Guardian*, Samuel Langford), Patrick McGuigan, Ena Mitchell, Nicholas Powell, Joseph Ward and Irene Wilde, with Betty Bannerman joining later.

Manduell and his staff introduced a new four-year undergraduate course. Provision was made for weekly double tutorials in all areas of principal study at undergraduate level, with triple provision for postgraduates. The French system of *solfège* ear training was introduced. All students of composition, orchestral instruments and singing were required to acquire keyboard competence. Other features were methodical language studies, a 'history of ideas' course, classes in style and interpretation and increased emphasis on chamber music and ensemble work. The first two years were to be devoted to a Part I course providing a broad education combined with intensive tuition in the student's principal subject. The Part II courses provided for specialisation to a high professional standard and could lead to advanced study at postgraduate level. A feature of Part II was classes designed to ensure that students knew how to attain confidence and ease of presentation on the concert platform. Options open to students showed the adventurous spirit abroad in the new College – jazz, film music and electronic music were in the curriculum, not as exotic eccentricities but accepted as part of the mainstream of twentieth century music in its final three decades. The students' union was accorded important recognition and by November 1973 a staff-student liaison committee had been formed.

The first intake of exclusively RNCM students, including postgraduates, numbered 87, a low figure reflecting shortage of time to publicise the College and to produce a prospectus. Concurrently, the courses of the RMCM and NSM were fully maintained until their completion in, respectively, 1976 and 1975. Where the RNCM students benefited in a way undreamed of by their predecessors was in the provision, under the direction of John Bower, of an elaborate and sophisticated range of recording facilities. Not only were these used as aural evidence for the benefit – or dismay! – of tutors and students, but they meant that an archive of all College activities was steadily being built up (its use to posterity can scarcely be gauged). Complementary to this was the development of the library under Anthony Hodges and Laura Birchall, not only its stock of books but recordings and tapes and a computer for cataloguing. Early bequests to the new College were the composer Alan Rawsthorne's manuscripts and the

John Bower, Recording Manager.

David Jordan with an early RNCM Symphony Orchestra.

eminent conductor Jascha Horenstein's conducting library.

The opening of the Royal Northern College of Music – a name, curiously, which had been suggested by Gustav Behrens as far back as 1893 when the nomenclature of what became the Royal Manchester College of Music was causing controversy – coincided with the stirrings generally of a Manchester renaissance. The Hallé Orchestra's quarter-century golden age under Sir John Barbirolli had ended with the great conductor's death in July 1970. Now it was beginning a new era under a young conductor, James Loughran. The 69 Theatre Company, under the direction of Michael Elliott, was about to move into the disused Royal Exchange, formerly the centre of Manchester's commercial life and wealth, where it built a novel theatre-in-the-round which was to attract fine actors and directors anxious to work in a fresh and stimulating atmosphere. Chetham's School, founded in 1656, had boldly turned itself in 1969 into a music school, offering a general education but with music as the principal subject for all pupils from the ages of 7 to 18. And, through the initiative of Raphael Gonley – a former student of the RMCM (as Beckmesser in that college's production of *Die Meistersinger* he had played his own lute!) and then employed by the BBC's Radio Manchester – a chamber orchestra, the Manchester Camerata, had been formed and was attracting loyal and large audiences. There was even talk of a regional opera company based in Manchester by 1973, but it was only talk and what is now the independent Opera North was founded in Leeds in 1978 as an outcrop of English National Opera.

The last concert to be given under the independent auspices of the RMCM was by members of the Junior School in July 1972. Its last student to register (No.6,038) was the organist Graham Barber in January 1973. The first internal concert by the new Northern College of Music was performed in the old RMCM building, when the programme included Grieg's violin sonata, Op.13, a favourite work of Sir Charles Hallé and of Adolph Brodsky, the first two Principals of the RMCM. Thus was tradition maintained. Events in the new College's Concert Hall were delayed by the after-effects of the building strike. So the inaugural concert of the First Orchestra was given in the large hall of Manchester Town Hall on 7 November 1972. In the first half David Jordan (RMCM) conducted Wagner's overture to *Die Meistersinger* and Maurice Clare (NSM) conducted Bliss's *Music for Strings*; and after the interval Charles Groves conducted Vaughan Williams's *A London Symphony*, after which honorary fellowship of the NSM was conferred on him. The Concert Hall was inaugurated on 15 November with an Invitation Concert, broadcast live on Radio 3 as part of the BBC's fiftieth anniversary celebrations. Elgar Howarth conducted the London Sinfonietta in works by the 'Manchester School', the three composers who, rather to the surprise of the RMCM, had emerged in the 1950s as student leaders of the *avant-garde*. In this programme were Harrison Birtwistle's *Verses for Ensemble*, Peter Maxwell Davies's *St Michael Sonata*, and *Three Pieces* for wind and percussion from Alexander Goehr's opera *Arden Must Die*. The pianist David Wilde played (on a Bösendorfer) Maxwell Davies's *5 Pieces*, op.2, and Goehr's *Nonomiya*. A voice cried 'Rubbish' at the end of the concert. Gerald Larner's verdict in *The Guardian* on the hall's acoustics was that, with so many seats empty, they 'seemed almost too lively, too resonant – by which I mean too loud, not over-reverberant. The sound is clear but … it is also uncomfortably close to the ear.' (Larner was to write just over a year later that the hall was 'just not suitable for large-scale orchestral music. The acoustic is so close that at the climaxes you cannot hear the music for the noise.') It was not until the early 1980s that the problem of the Concert Hall's acoustics was, if not solved, considerably eased by various technical adjustments. On 16 November Karin Krog, a jazz singer, and Richard Rodney Bennett performed works by Joplin, Cage and Bennett himself.

Manduell's policy of providing a wide range of concerts and other events as a 'vital adjunct to the teaching programme' was instituted immediately. It had always been part of the thinking behind the new college that it should also serve as an Arts Centre for Manchester. On the second day, 9 January, of the first term in the new building, the baritone Thomas Hemsley, accompanied by David Wilde, gave a Schubert recital in the Concert Hall. Eight days later another baritone, John Shirley-Quirk, with Martin Isepp as accompanist, sang cycles by Vaughan Williams, Finzi and Britten, following them two evenings later with Schubert's *Winterreise*. On 23 January the Allegri Quartet played Schubert's 'Death and the Maiden' Quartet and was joined by William Pleeth for the C major Quintet. The College's Chamber Orchestra, directed by Raphael Sommer, and the Second Orchestra, conducted by David Jordan, both gave concerts during February, but the chief event was the inauguration – lasting the best part of four hours – of the Opera Theatre on 20, 22 and 24 February with the double bill of Crosse's *Purgatory* and Walton's *The Bear* preceded (on the first night only) by *Belshazzar's Feast*. John Wray conducted the Walton choral work, with Alexander Gauld as baritone soloist. Names in the chorus which are now well known were Rita Cullis, Diana Montague, Henry Herford, Phillip Joll, Mark Richardson, Christopher Underwood and Graham Vick. *Purgatory* was produced by James Maxwell of the 69 Theatre Company and conducted by Michael

Glenville Hargreaves as the Old Man, Carole Brooksbank as the Spirit of the Old Man's Mother in Purgatory by Gordon Crosse - one of the inaugural productions in February 1973.

Lankester, with Glenville Hargreaves as the Old Man. (This production achieved a College 'first' in being commercially recorded, Crosse insisting that the College cast could not be bettered.) The Walton 'extravaganza', based on Chekhov, was conducted by Bryden Thomson, produced by Ernest Warburton of the BBC and had John Rawnsley as the 'bear' of the title, Smirnov. In the first interval there was a lengthy reception and in the interval between the operas the students presented 'A Bawdy Cabaret (with apologies to Purcell)' on the Concourse. On 26 February the organ in the Concert Hall was inaugurated by Geraint Jones, whose recital included works by Boyce, Stanley, Couperin, Dandrieu, Daquin, J.S. Bach, Seixas and Liszt.

One of the two pianists in the Second Orchestra's performance of Saint-Saëns's *Carnival of the Animals* on 30 March was Peter Donahoe (as he was mis-spelt) and the soloist in Brahms's D minor Piano Concerto with the First Orchestra on 3 April was Martin Roscoe. Both these concerts were conducted by David Jordan who on 13 March had already conducted the First Orchestra in Strauss's *Ein Heldenleben*. The pianists Donohoe and Roscoe, good friends today who often play duets together, were encouraged to regard each other as rivals, Roscoe being held up to Donohoe as an example of true diligence. Donohoe was one of the most interesting personalities among the early intake. He had been a pupil at Chetham's for five years before it became a music school. An only child who had showed an early aptitude for the piano, he was acutely aware of his parents' ambition for him to be an international virtuoso. He was at the College from 1972 to 1976 and admits that he was a 'contrary' individual, naturally subversive. His interest was not in being a solo pianist but in playing chamber music or being in an orchestra as a percussionist or pianist. At their first meeting Manduell asked him if he was serious about his percussion playing and why. Because there's a job at the end, he replied – and was conscious he was regarded as doing the wrong thing. Donohoe believed then – and does still – that College policy was primarily to encourage specialisation for a glamorous career and that the discouragement of pianists from a second-study instrument was wrong – 'dumping a safety net', he called it – because encouraging participation in chamber music, accompanying, orchestral playing, composition and jazz would in no way impede development as a soloist.

Donohoe's guide and teacher, to whom he feels he owes so much, was Derrick Wyndham, a stern taskmaster who was the right man for a student who had large holes in his technique because of his reluctance to practise: he preferred to be rehearsing as drummer for the first concert of the Big Band when it was formed, playing the side-drum (as he did in *Ein Heldenleben*), or slipping over to Liverpool to play in the RLPO percussion section. Even when he left the College in 1976, he would rather have been a timpanist in an orchestra than a solo pianist. But a Hallé engagement within a few weeks of graduation changed all that. Today he regards the College with affection and says:'I would want it to be as it was if I had to do it again.'

An RMCM occasion in the Concert Hall on 21 March was a tribute by four of her former students to the singing teacher Elsie Thurston who entered the RMCM as a student in 1913 and was on its staff from 1921 to 1972. Elizabeth Harwood, Honor Sheppard, Barbara Robotham and Marjorie Thomas marked her retirement with an evening of memorable singing. The College's first full-scale opera production was Britten's *A Midsummer Night's Dream*, produced by Joseph Ward, who had created the role of Starveling at Aldeburgh in 1960 (and on that occasion had also sung Demetrius from the pit on the first night because Thomas Hemsley had lost his voice). The recently-knighted Charles Groves conducted two of the three performances (23 and 26 May; Jordan conducted on the 25th) and the assistant producer was Graham Vick. Some of the roles were double-cast; thus, Glenville Hargreaves and John Rawnsley shared Demetrius. The Tytania was Vida Schepens. Although the lighting designer was Keith Hubbard, it was controlled by Philip L. Edwards who thereafter was the College's chief electrician and lighting designer. His association with RNCM opera productions continues today.

The performances were part of the College's contribution to a Manchester Festival, as were two recitals on 29 and 31 May of Prokofiev's piano sonatas, played by Antoni Brozak, Alicja Fiderkiewicz, David Hartigan and Czeslaw Pytel. The festival brought two other organisations into the College – the Northern Dance Theatre gave the first of several seasons of ballet there and the Manchester Camerata gave the last festival concert on 2 June, including the first performance of David Ellis's *Solus*. The summer term ended with two concerts. The first, on 30 June, was given by members of the Junior School, among whom one notes the pianists John Gough, Sally Ann Bottomley and Penelope Roskell. On 3 July, Jordan conducted the First Orchestra in three Shostakovich works, ending with the Fifth Symphony.

Kate Flowers as Helena and John Rawnsley as Demetrius in Joseph Ward's 1973 production of Britten's A Midsummer Night's Dream.

The Principal with the Polish Ambassador after the unveiling of the statue of Chopin by Ludwika Nitschowa in October 1973. Photograph courtesy John Rawnsley

III *A New Style*

When the next term began in September 1973 – the first RNCM academic session – the College's elevation to 'Royal' status was reflected by the new style of its printed programmes and other documentation, very pleasing to the eye and, indeed, stylish. The College philosophy was that what it did should not only sound good but look good in every respect. This elegance was owed to Keith Murgatroyd, who was the College's design consultant from its inception until his retirement over a decade later. The handily-sized brochures listing activities at the College for the rest of 1973 showed how rapidly the new Concert Hall and Opera Theatre had been seized upon by extra-collegiate organisations. Manchester Camerata gave its Saturday concerts in the College. Manchester Chamber Concerts Society monthly concerts moved there. The BBC Northern Symphony Orchestra, as the BBC Philharmonic was then called, gave its Friday Midday Proms there. Other visitors included the Northern Dance Theatre, the Hungarian State Puppet Theatre, the Kodály Quartet, Nash Ensemble, Ulster Orchestra and London Sinfonietta. A concert was devoted to the music of Berio. On 24 September the College's first London promotion was a Wigmore Hall recital by selected senior students.

In mid-October, the Polish Ambassador unveiled a full-length statue of Chopin by Ludwika Nitschowa which had been given to the College by the Chopin Society of Warsaw to mark the 125th anniversary of the recital Chopin gave in Manchester on his last visit to Britain. It stands on the Concourse and shows the great man huddled in a cloak as if expecting Manchester's weather to live down to its reputation. Later in the day the Polish pianist Ryszard Bakst, a distinguished member of the School of Keyboard Studies, played Chopin mazurkas and polonaises and the F minor concerto with the First Orchestra, conducted by Jordan. On the previous day John Wray and Jordan, with various soloists, conducted a programme of his own music in honour of the revered composer and composition professor Thomas Pitfield, who had retired earlier in the year after many years also on the RMCM staff.

Four opera productions were staged during this term. Three were revivals – *Purgatory, The Bear* and *A Midsummer Night's Dream* – and the fourth, on 4 and 6 December, was Stravinsky's *The Rake's Progress*, conducted by Elgar Howarth and produced by Anthony Besch. It was not without significance for the College's image that so far it had tackled only operas composed in the twentieth century. In the Stravinsky, Anne Trulove was sung by Miriam Bowen, Tom Rakewell by Nigel Robson, and Nick Shadow by Glenville Hargreaves. Undoubtedly this opera was chosen by Alexander Young, Stravinsky's own favourite tenor as Tom and who recorded it under the composer's direction. The operas were taken to Sadler's Wells Theatre from 11 to 15 December, the double bill being performed once, the others twice. Comments in the press were highly complimentary. For instance, Joan Chissell in *The Times* on the Britten:

> It quickly became difficult to remember that these were in fact students. Visually, dramatically and musically the performance had a sense of style and atmosphere making it as enjoyable as any you could wish to see … London conservatories will have to look to their laurels if this is what comes out of Manchester.

Discussing *The Rake's Progress* in the *Financial Times*, Andrew Porter wrote of Manduell and his staff 'working some marvels in Manchester' and described the chorus as

> … one of the finest opera choruses it has ever been my delight to encounter, strong and clear in tone, precise in attack and in chording and splendid actors all, moving with an ease, a naturalness and an absence of fuss seldom seen on the professional stage.

Stanley Sadie described it in *The Times* as 'on every level just about the most accomplished student performance of any opera I can remember hearing'.

Today it seems a natural process that the College should have been so quick to launch itself in London and invite comparison with other colleges and professional companies. Yet how well I remember some of the scoffing that was heard in some quarters in Manchester – the place and its Principal had ideas above their station; the College was neglecting its duty as a teaching establishment in order to pursue publicity from extra-curricular activities; it was nothing but an arts centre (and what was wrong with that, most sensible people would ask). Spiky criticism of the College's academic syllabus, its appointments and its building came particularly from Richard Witts, a 23-year-old percussionist who was administrator of Normedia, a now-defunct modern music group in Manchester. The press comment on the Sadler's Wells season was in itself sufficient answer to the doubters and brought the College's first calendar year to an end on a high note. Yet the high levels of pay at the College and its

Glenville Hargreaves (left) as Nick Shadow and Nigel Robson as Tom Rakewell in Stravinsky's The Rake's Progress in December 1973. Photograph: Photocall Manchester

generous budget, for which the local authorities, whatever their occasional gripes, were responsible, was a cause of jealousy in other establishments and musical organisations which undoubtedly believed that Manduell was encouraged to be extravagant, little though they thought he needed such encouragement. But when economies were eventually required, the College had sufficient fat to shed before any bone was reached.

After the excitement and the 'firsts' of 1973, it was inevitable that 1974 should be a year of consolidation. Public lectures crept into the schedule and proved popular, not surprisingly when they included Sheila Barlow on 'non-verbal communication', showing how 'body language' on stage should be part of a singer's training, and Henri Pousseur discussing his music in advance of a concert devoted to it. Later lecturers, if such a prosaic term can be applied to them, were Isobel Baillie, Eva Turner, Peter Hemmings, Joyce Grenfell and Antony Hopkins. Regular exhibitions of works of art in various media were held on the Concourse – painting, sculpture, handiwork, and weaving. John Cage's *Musicircus* was performed, if that is the word; Hermann Prey gave a *Lieder* recital; the music of Varèse had a concert to itself performed by Saar Radio Symphony Orchestra; Maxwell Davies directed his Fires of London in his own music and in a work by Birtwistle. On 12 February the First Orchestra gave its first concert under its new title of RNCM Symphony Orchestra. Steve Reich and his Musicians performed his *Drumming*. Vlado Perlemuter, who came to the College as visiting tutor in pianoforte repertoire, gave a recital of Bach, Chopin, Debussy and Ravel.

On 19 March the College's Student Travel Scholarship Fund, to provide financial help to students undertaking approved holiday projects, was formally established at an inaugural recital by Cecil Aronowitz (viola) and Nicola Grunberg (piano). Other recitals supporting the fund followed, the first being by the guitarist John Williams. The Schoenberg centenary was marked in May by four BBC recitals in the Concert Hall at which the Dartington Quartet performed the four string quartets. Each was preceded by a talk by the musicologist Hans Keller. When the *Daily Telegraph* critic W.R. Sinclair mildly and humorously complained in print that the talks lasted far longer than the music, he received a savage (and humourless) complaint from Keller.

Again, four new opera productions were presented during the year. In March Robert Elliott directed (from the harpsichord) Monteverdi's *Il Combattimento di Tancredi e Clorinda* and Purcell's *Dido and Aeneas*. Dennis Arundell was the producer, continuing the College's policy of inviting established and experienced

The Duchess of Kent talking to students during one of her many visits to the College. Sir Charles Groves and pianist John Ogdon can be seen in the background. Photograph: Lawrence Photographers

professionals to work with the students. In May, Geza Partós produced the first British staging for 50 years of Massenet's *Thaïs*, conducted by David Jordan, with Mary Conway in the title-role and Glenville Hargreaves as Athanael. Also in the cast were Robin Leggate and Diana Montague. In December the young conductor Richard Hickox made his début in opera in the College's *Aida*, produced by Arthur Hammond, designed by Juanita Waterson and involving over 250 performers. This, too, was ecstatically reviewed. There were two casts, in one of which an Australian mezzo-soprano Rachel Gettler sang Amneris, Janet Evans sang Aida, John Rawnsley was Amonasro, Lanceford Roberts the Radames and Phillip Joll the Ramphis.

The Opera Theatre was increasingly in demand by non-college companies. During 1974 Northern Dance Theatre continued its association with the RNCM and was emulated by London Contemporary Dance Theatre (who performed an item called *A Waterless Method of Swimming Instruction*) and the Prospect Theatre Company, who performed Shakespeare's *Henry IV Parts 1 and 2* and *Henry V*. Manchester Opera Company in April staged Verdi's *The Force of Destiny*.

The enterprise of the College's own orchestra was epitomised when Jordan conducted Mahler's Fifth Symphony in July. In June the Principal's Concerts, at which senior students display their talent, were inaugurated. Proceeds from these concerts are shared between the participating students, all of whom will have just completed their RNCM studies, to give them financial help at the start of their careers. More prosaic but no less important events were the new status, with significantly improved salaries, established for all part-time members of the academic staff and the formal inauguration, on 19 November, of the Association of Friends, which had of course been in existence since 1971. On 11 December, the Duchess of Kent presided at the first annual Congregation of Awards and conferred Honorary Fellowships on Ida Carroll, Philip Cranmer (then professor of music at the University of Manchester), Terence Greaves, Sir Charles Groves, Sir Anthony Lewis (Principal of the Royal Academy of Music), John Manduell and John Wray. She herself was similarly honoured. The College was enabled to realise how fortunate it was to have the Duchess as President. A keen pianist, a member of the Bach Choir, a regular opera-goer who is not shy to admit that she threw flowers on to the Covent Garden stage at Plácido Domingo's curtain-calls, she is an active and involved President, deeply interested in everything affecting the College and immensely proud of it. At all her many visits, she has thrown timetables into confusion by her insistence on talking to as many students as possible. After any performance she attends, she goes backstage to visit the performers and every recipient of a diploma or prize at the graduation ceremony each December is greeted and clasped as warmly as if he or she had just won the Men's or Women's singles final at Wimbledon. Typical of her attitude was her response to Manduell's suggestion, after she had been in poor health, that she could reduce the strain of the Congregation of Awards by pronouncing a 'blanket' conferment instead of giving each individual student his or her diploma with the statutory spoken commendation. She refused, saying that this was each graduate's 'big day' and she would not diminish it in any respect.

Sir Charles Groves rehearses the RNCM Symphony Orchestra.

IV Court and Council

The most far-reaching event of 1974 was the sealing on 30 June by the Secretary of State for Education of the Instruments and Articles of Government of the College. This paved the way for the replacement of the Joint Committee by a Court and Council. These bodies were formally established during 1975. The Court held the purse-strings and took final decisions and was dominated by local authority members (16 out of 24). The other members were representatives of the RMCM and NSM. The Council's responsibility was the academic work of the College and its day-to-day running. Although local authority members were on the Council, they were outnumbered by members from music, the arts and education. The Court first met on 22 July under the chairmanship of Dame Kathleen Ollerenshaw, who happily was Lord Mayor of Manchester in this year. Its membership included two men whose names were writ large in Manchester's musical tradition, Sir Leonard Behrens, a former Hallé chairman whose father Gustav had been one of the three men who ensured the continuation of the Hallé concerts after Hallé's death and played a major role in establishing the RMCM, and Richard Godlee, whose father Philip, as chairman of the Hallé in 1943, had sent for Barbirolli. The Council first met on 6 November 1975. Its chairman was Sir Charles Groves, with Simon Towneley as vice-chairman. Among its 26 other members were Ida Carroll, John Wray, Dame Kathleen, John Manduell, Sir Denis

Philip Jones (left), first Head of Wind and Percussion, with his successor Timothy Reynish.

Forman of Granada TV, the composers and professors Alexander Goehr (Leeds University), William Mathias (University College of North Wales, Bangor), and Basil Deane (Manchester University), representatives of the College staff and the president of the students' union.

In the concert schedule, the College Big Band, directed by Keiron Anderson, made its début in the Concert Hall on 7 March with Peter Donohoe as the drummer. Four days later Donohoe, who in the previous October had been soloist in Bartók's second concerto, gave a recital of Bartók and Ravel which led Paul Dewhirst to write in the *Daily Telegraph* that 'no student instrumentalist I have heard at the RNCM has made a greater impression and, luck permitting, seems more likely to make an international career'. The Northern Dance Theatre continued its seasonal visits and for a week from 27 January the Royal Shakespeare Company staged Marlowe's *Dr Faustus* with Ian McKellen in the title-role. On 11, 13 and 15 February Manchester Opera Company performed Verdi's *Otello*, notable for the singing of the name-part by an unknown tenor, Jeffrey Lawton, who some years later was to sing the role for Welsh National Opera in Peter Stein's famous production and to sing Tristan at Covent Garden in another WNO production. When the Fitzwilliam Quartet played in the Recital Room on 5 March, it gave the British première of Shostakovich's fifteenth string quartet. The growing co-operation with Chetham's School was marked by the appearance of the school's chamber choir and senior orchestra in a concert in the Concert Hall on 15 March.

The College held its first graduation ball on 25 June 1975 and at the start of the summer term the vacant position of Head of the School of Wind and Percussion was filled by the trumpeter Philip Jones, well known for his concerts with the Philip Jones Brass Ensemble. An audio-visual film of the work of the College was submitted (through the agency of Keith Murgatroyd) to the Royal Society of Arts for one of its presidential awards in design management. It was selected for the Duke of Edinburgh's award, which was presented by the Duke himself, president of the RSA, at the Society's London headquarters in November.

The first concert to be given at the RNCM by visiting overseas students was on 23 September 1975, when music by Sibelius, Englund, Palmgren, Bach, Brouwer, Dowland and Vaughan Williams was performed by a mezzo-soprano, two pianists, an organist and a guitarist from the Sibelius Academy of Helsinki. Concerts by the College Symphony Orchestra included performances of Lennox Berkeley's Third Symphony and Strauss's *Also sprach Zarathustra*. At the concert on 29 October the soloist in Grieg's concerto was a piano student, David Fanning, who later joined the University Music Department's teaching staff and contributed music reviews to *The Guardian, The Independent* and *Gramophone*. He is not the only person associated with the College to have entered the world of music criticism. The assistant librarian from 1985, Geoffrey Thomason, whose comprehensive programme-notes distinguish the College's programmes, also writes for *The Guardian*, and for a brief period Geoffrey Norris of the *Daily Telegraph* was a tutor in the School of Theory and Humanities. Other new members of this school between 1973 and 1975 were Colin Beeson, Douglas Jarman, Peter Syrus, David Young and Michel Brandt.

Ravel's centenary had been marked during May by a series of events, including a photographic exhibition, a piano recital by Pascal Rogé, a song-recital and master classes by Gérard Souzay, and performances of his opera *L'heure espagnole* in a double bill with Falla's *Master Peter's Puppet Show*, both conducted by Jordan, the former produced by Patrick Libby, the latter by the College's lecturer in Opera Studies, Malcolm Fraser, who added a mimed prologue 'apparently,' wrote Gerald Larner, 'on the assumption that we have never heard of Don Quixote.' The concert by the Symphony Orchestra under Jordan on 27 June comprising Bartók's Second Violin Concerto and Berlioz's *Symphonie Fantastique* was repeated the next evening in the Philharmonic Hall, Liverpool, a first foray into wider territory. A new departure in the Opera Theatre was the showing of films of opera productions, for example of *Fidelio, The Threepenny Opera, Wozzeck* and *Die Meistersinger von Nürnberg*. Ensembles such as Swingle II, The Fires of London and The Scholars appeared at the College. The emphasis on *avant-garde* and contemporary music was strong. In not many other venues at this time could one hear the works of Kagel, Bosseur and Pousseur, to name only three. On 1 December students of the Belgrade Academy inaugurated an annual exchange with Jugoslav students. *Aida* was revived and on 17 December Sir Charles Groves conducted the Symphony Orchestra in Mahler's *Das Lied von der Erde*, with Rachel Gettler and Robin Leggate as the mezzo and tenor soloists, a performance that one critic described as the RNCM's 'finest achievement to date'. And who that was present will easily forget the late Cathy Berberian's panorama of 'Revolutions in Music' in a programme ranging from Monteverdi and Offenbach to Cage, Berio and Lennon and McCartney?

The year 1976 was one in which Britain's economic health was yet again on the danger list. Speaking on 18 February at the second Congregation of Awards, at which the Duchess of Kent became the first Companion of the College, Manduell took comfort from a Government Minister's pronouncement that 'there is

From left to right: Keith Mills as Torquemada, Olga Gracelj as Concepcion and Phillip Joll as Ramiro in the 1975 production of Ravel's L'heure espagnole, which also toured to Denmark in 1976.

nothing particularly élitist, only realistic, about policies which make proper provision for the early specialist development of youngsters with indisputable potential when to do otherwise would be to shirk an inescapable responsibility' Yet Manduell sensed that cuts in education budgets, if they continued, might leave Britain 'the least well-educated' nation in Europe as well as the poorest. 'We must not as a nation run the risk of emasculating the rarer examples of significant potential and unusual calibre when these appear. We must acknowledge that we hold in trust as a sacred responsibility the development of those with precious gifts. That responsibility cannot be honourably discharged if it is obliged to bend to any prescription which inevitably encourages mediocrity.' The doctrine of the Court and Council was that, come what may, nothing should compromise the College's high standards. Local government representatives often found it hard to understand this refusal to lower standards to accommodate economies, but many of them had to their credit developed a great pride in the College and went along with the Principal's lofty conception of its role, a conception well supported by the growing list of RNCM students who won international and national prizes and competitions. The recipients of Honorary Fellowships in 1976 were Sir Lennox Berkeley, James Loughran and Dr Kenneth Barritt, Principal of the Royal Scottish Academy of Music and Drama and, from the College staff, Sheila Barlow, Clifton Helliwell and Dorothy Pilling.

As if to emphasise its determination to avoid mediocrity, the RNCM in March gave two performances apiece of the four one-act operas it had so far staged. Crosse's *Purgatory* was revived in a new production by Malcolm Fraser, designed by Michael Holt and conducted by Timothy Reynish, a recent recruit to the teaching staff. He also conducted *The Bear* while Jordan retained the Falla and Ravel. The season was a preliminary to a tour of Scandinavia from 24 March to 8 April in which five opera performances were given in the Royal Opera House, Copenhagen, with three of the productions also staged in Aalborg. The symphony orchestra also gave five concerts in Åarhus, Copenhagen, Esbjerg, Göteborg and Odense. All were conducted by Jordan who chose two programmes, the first containing Berkeley's Third Symphony and Mahler's *Das Lied von der Erde*, the second a Haydn symphony, Prokofiev's Third Piano Concerto (soloist Christopher Green-Armytage) and Strauss's *Ein Heldenleben*. The first night of the opera season in Copenhagen was attended by the British Ambassador and by the Lord Mayor of Manchester, who of course just happened still to be Dame Kathleen Ollerenshaw.

v Stars – and Shadows

At the start of 1976, the College had been granted its armorial bearings. To describe them, I resort to John Manduell's report for 1975-6:

> The shield symbolises a northern music establishment based on four areas, and the crest specifies the College's origins and royal title. The shield is quartered red and blue; the red is the background of the arms of the City of Manchester and Lancashire County Council, and the blue is that of the arms of the City of Salford and Cheshire County Council. A golden lyre … refers not only to musical studies but is also an emblem of Apollo, patron of the Muses, and a reminder that other cultural activities are to be found at the College. Above the lyre a white irradiated star represents the Northern Star, in allusion to the College's title. Above the shield is the closed helm proper to civic and corporate arms, with its crest-wreath and flowing mantle in the main colours of the shield, red, blue, and gold, which combine the heraldic liveries of all four authorities. On the wreath is the crest. The lion is a supporter of the arms of Manchester and also of the Royal Arms, and wears a crown in allusion to the Royal title. Round its neck is a garland of sallow leaves from the heraldic badge of Salford, and the lion is encircled by red roses from the Lancashire County Council shield and gold oak leaves from the heraldic badge of Cheshire County Council. To complete the symbolism, the lion holds a music score.

The College's motto is *Fovet musica omnes* – Music enriches all.

During 1976 Simon Towneley, vice-chairman of the College Council, was appointed Lord Lieutenant of Lancashire, and Ida Carroll, Dean of Management, became president of the Incorporated Society of Musicians which held its annual conference at the RNCM in April 1977 (when Sir David Willcocks, then Director of the Royal College of Music, won a snooker tournament). Miss Carroll retired from her College post on 31 August 1976. As a tribute to this 'true professional', as Sir Charles Groves called her, the College established in her name its first research fellowship.

On the day – 7 December 1976 – that she formally opened Hartley Hall, the Duchess of Kent in the evening attended the première of the first opera to be commissioned by the RNCM. This was *Stars and Shadows*, music by Brian Hughes, chorusmaster at the College, who conducted, and libretto by Ursula

Vaughan Williams. It was in one act and was performed in a double bill with a production by Euan Smith of Vaughan Williams's *Riders to the Sea*. The new work was a light-hearted affair about auditions for a pantomime and used a large cast. 'The scoring is light, the style eclectic,' Elizabeth Forbes wrote in the *Financial Times*. Among the singers were Hugh Hetherington, Vanessa Williamson, Mark Curtis, Robin Martin-Oliver, and Robert Dean. *Riders to the Sea* was conducted by Andrew Penny, with Maria Jagus as Maurya.

The year 1977 opened with a Congregation of Awards on 25 January at which the Duchess conferred Honorary Fellowship on Sir David Willcocks and on five College stalwarts, Ena Mitchell, Cecil Aronowitz, Philip Jones, Simon Towneley and Alexander Young. But there was a sombre note to the proceedings. In his report on the previous year, Manduell touched on

> the material deterioration in the national situation … Economists have demonstrated all too clearly our lowly position in the European economic league tables, while educationists have revealed the alarming rise in illiteracy … Can we [at the RNCM] claim that we have avoided prescriptions which encourage mediocrity or that we have successfully resisted tendencies which make it the harder for us honourably and effectively to discharge our responsibilities as guardians of scholarship or trustees of precious skills? I make a plea that those in positions of central authority in education should devote themselves to renewing the bright fires of faith and conviction rather than allowing the dull embers of expediency and compromise to emasculate still further a deteriorating position …
>
> … It is evident that our responsibility between now and 1983 is likely to be to accommodate more rather than fewer undergraduate students … In the meantime our problem is likely to be to meet a higher demand than at present with a reduced teaching capacity necessitated by the requirement to widen our staff-student ratio. In a discipline which calls for such a high and intensive degree of individual teaching as music inevitably requires, this combination will impose very severe strain on our resources and capacity. Intelligent redeployment of resources can offer us part of the answer, no doubt … But after redeployment there are few alternative steps which would be open to us before we found ourselves obliged to exclude rather than reduce any given tutorial provision. If this College is to maintain its position as one of the leading conservatoires, it must ensure that it is in a position to exclude such exclusion.

Manduell also said that the College's ability to help students hard-pressed for fees had been dramatically reduced by the ravages of inflation on the funds available for such purposes. He criticised the Government for choosing this moment, 'the worst conceivable', to propose steep increases in fees, while 'it is unfortunate that at the same time the old unpopular differentiation between fees for undergraduate and for postgraduate students and between fees for home and for overseas students has been retained … None of us can with a clear conscience subscribe to policies or practices which render opportunities in education beyond the grasp of those who otherwise merit and qualify for them.'

Another exchange visit materialised on 21 January 1977 when Danish students from the Royal Academy of Music in Åarhus performed new works for percussion by Kagel, Stockhausen and Haubenstock-Ramati, among others. The following evening Manduell made one of his rare appearances as a conductor when the College Chamber Orchestra played a programme of Mozart, Weber, Dvořák and David Gill. On 1 March Peter Donohoe, now launched on his career, returned to give a recital ranging from Mozart to Messiaen via Scriabin and Liszt. In the *Daily Telegraph*, Paul Dewhirst amusingly began his notice: 'Although I am not acquainted with the RNCM students' union junior common room, it must surely by now be uncommonly well appointed to judge by the number of recitals that have been given to raise funds for it.'

The chief event this spring was the opera season from 8 to 17 March when the Royal Danish Academy, Copenhagen, brought a double bill of Gluck's *Le Cinesi* and Nørholm's *The Garden Wall*, a RDAM commission receiving its first performance. The RNCM mounted a new production of *La Bohème*, in which Neville Marriner made his début as an opera conductor. Joseph Ward produced. All three operas became part of another Sadler's Wells season from 15 March to 2 April when the RNCM added its double bill of *Stars and Shadows* (revised since its première) and *Riders to the Sea* and the London Opera Centre performed Lully's *Alceste* and Britten's *The Rape of Lucretia*. The *Bohème* casts had Lanceford Roberts as Rodolfo, Janet Gration and Patricia Byrne as Mimi, Olga Gracelj as Musetta and Phillip Joll as Marcello. The London critics generally felt that this was not up to the standard of previous RNCM offerings. 'There is no substitute in Puccini for good voices,' Ronald Crichton wrote in the *Financial Times*. 'The first two acts … were a hearty rough and tumble, with the singers warming up and Neville Marriner … firmly in control but so brisk and breezy that lyricism hardly peeped round the corner.' But Anthony Payne in the *Daily Telegraph* thought the 'freshness and ardour' brought to the score by the students 'overrode

A party for Cecil Aronowitz, first Head of Strings, who is seen in the foreground, left, with his successor, Eleanor Warren, and John Manduell. String tutors and senior academic staff in the background are, left to right: Clifton Helliwell, Atar Arad, Patrick Ireland, Maurice Clare, Terence Greaves, Philip Jones, Clifford Knowles, Terence Weil, Walter Jorysz, Rudolf Botta, Dr John Wray, Alexander Young.

all other considerations ... Joseph Ward's production was spontaneous and fresh.' Philip Hope-Wallace in *The Guardian* found the third act 'perfect in pace and texture ... I could not fault a thing.'

The Opera Theatre in Manchester was in use from 4 to 9 April when Scottish Opera visited the city for the first time, performing Verdi's *Macbeth* and Lehár's *The Merry Widow* in the Opera House and Mozart's *The Magic Flute* and Britten's *The Turn of the Screw* at the RNCM. This was the first time a professional opera company had used the Opera Theatre. During the summer term Simon Rattle conducted the Nash Ensemble on 22 June in a double bill of Stravinsky's *The Soldier's Tale* and John Tavener's *A Gentle Spirit* (based on Dostoevsky) with Elise Ross and Kenneth Woollam as soprano and tenor soloists. In July Chetham's School's director of music, Michael Brewer, conducted two performances of Elgar's Cello Concerto and Walton's *Belshazzar's Feast*. Among the artists who visited the College to give recitals in the autumn were the sopranos Elizabeth Harwood and Elisabeth Söderström, the Vermeer Quartet, and the organist Gillian Weir; and there were the regular concerts by Manchester Camerata, then conducted by Szymon Goldberg, the College Symphony Orchestra and the William Byrd Singers who, under Stephen Wilkinson, had won an enviable reputation in choral music of five centuries. In December an opera triple bill was staged: Stephen Oliver conducted his *The Waiter's Revenge*; Richard Vardigans conducted the première of *The Time Killing* by Alison Cox, a fourth-year composition student at the RNCM; and Jane Glover conducted Haydn's *Deceit Outwitted (L'infedeltà delusa)* in a stylish production by Malcolm Fraser and with Deborah Rees and Mark Curtis in the cast. Another composition student at this time, a pupil of Anthony Gilbert, was Sally Beamish, who was also a violist.

Three staff changes occurred during 1977. In May, David Jordan became Director of Opera Studies in succession to Joseph Ward, who was Assistant Head of the School of Vocal Studies, and in August Eleanor Warren, Head of Music Programmes at the BBC, and a distinguished cellist, became Head of the School of Strings in succession to Cecil Aronowitz, who went to the Britten-Pears School at Snape and died in 1978. Also in August, Timothy Reynish, who since 1975 had been tutor in charge of the postgraduate conducting course, became Head of the School of Wind and Percussion. He succeeded Philip Jones.

But the most significant feature of 1977 was that it marked the completion of the first four-year undergraduate course and the introduction of a revised course structure. Alternative courses were developed, the most important of which was the Associate (or Professional) Course. The College now offered several academic awards: GMusRNCM (Graduate in Music) with full Honours status, GRNCM (graduate) with Pass Degree status, PPRNCM (diploma in professional performance), and Performers' Laureate. There was also the Joint Course whereby MusB candidates of Manchester University could study concurrently for the College awards. The RNCM planned a Faculty of Advanced Studies for courses in affiliation with the university, leading to the award of MusM (Manchester) or a postgraduate diploma (Manchester). This was finally established on 1 September 1979, when five students were admitted to read for the MusM degree and 15 for the Diploma.

Typical of the College's seriousness of purpose was the series of four organ recitals on successive evenings in January 1978 at which Gillian Weir played the complete works of Messiaen for the instrument. It was a bold venture of a kind that had brought the RNCM international fame. What the College had achieved in five years was admirably summed up in an article Hugo Cole wrote for *Country Life* (5 January 1978). This was a candid, clear-sighted view of the RNCM and is worth extensive quotation. Entering the building, Cole said,

> you instinctively look for the arrivals and departures board. An architect's dream of a music college, in which human figures seem almost irrelevant … Teachers and students endure ordeal by fire – more precisely, by central heating. As costs rose during the building, someone decided that money could be saved on the air circulation system. As a result, temperatures still vary alarmingly, according to the position of rooms and the vagaries of the system, between near-freezing and 79 °F. String players, in self-defence, equip their instruments with humidifiers …
>
> Opera is taken seriously at the RNCM … it was good to find that the two small-scale chamber operas which I saw on December 7 had been prepared with thoroughly professional care for detail in every department – singing, acting, instrumental performance, sets and lighting – something one all too rarely finds in professional, let alone student, productions … I was suitably impressed by the fully-equipped recording studio … and by the big library with table space for outsize avant-garde scores and listening points for records and cassettes. But the names on the doors of the teaching rooms were perhaps the most impressive thing of all. The RNCM … draws on teachers from all over Europe, and most of all from London, with many of the staff still commuting to Manchester every week. Thus the composition department has Anthony Gilbert as tutor in composition (resident in Manchester) with

Petr Eben (centre) at a reception for him during his year as Visiting Fellow in Composition.

Maxwell Davies as a regular visiting tutor, Sir William Glock as tutor laureatus – a curious title which might lead one to think that the big names were there to add lustre to the prospectus. But the day I was there Sir William was coaching an excellent string trio in Beethoven's opus 3. A live contact had been made; a wind had blown in from the outside world.

The RNCM aims to be rather more like a university music department than a conventional conservatoire, and is more outward-looking and conscious of its public role than any other conservatoire or university department that I know of … Students at the RNCM receive two hours' individual tuition each week in their principal study, and to judge from the prospectus, are not expected to skip out of college for the rest of the week, cutting their aurals and history classes, only going to hear fellow-pianists, violinists, or singers, as many brilliant students have done in the past … Better, all the same, to be over-stimulated rather than under-stimulated.

Cole was right to be impressed by the names on the doors. Sir Charles Groves was adviser in conducting studies; the Czech composer Petr Eben, who was lecturer in music at Charles University, Prague, spent a year as Visiting Fellow in composition; additions to the keyboard staff were Sulamita Aronovsky, a distinguished Russian teacher, and Renna Kellaway (Mrs Manduell); the assistant to Eleanor Warren as Head of the School of Strings was Patrick Ireland and among the tutors were Eli Goren, Bronislaw Gimpel, Ralph Kirshbaum, Moray Welsh, and Terence Weil (organiser of chamber music); the baritones Thomas Hemsley, John Cameron and Christopher Underwood joined the School of Vocal Studies, with the countertenor Alfred Deller as Visiting Tutor in Renaissance and Baroque studies; in the School of Wind and Percussion, Reynish's staff now included the trumpeter John Dickinson and the trombonist John Iveson. In the clerical staff at this date Sidney Palmer was bursar (affectionately remembered by one distinguished former student as 'a smashing old stick'), Bryan Fox was accommodation officer, Philip Jones the promotions co-ordinator, and Judy Watt had succeeded Olivia Maxwell as publicity officer.

On 6 March 1978, David Jordan conducted the first four performances of *Das Rheingold*, the first Wagner opera to be performed by the College. Wotan was sung by Phillip Joll, Alberich by Robert Dean, Fricka by Yvonne Lea, and Loge by Keith Mills. These singers all received high praise, especially for their German diction, as did the orchestra, enlarged to 110 players. But Euan Smith's production was described in the *Daily Telegraph* as the sort that has, alas, become a Wagnerian cliché of our day … The staging – circular raised platform and black curtains all round – is distracting and cumbersome: scene-shifting in public is a noisy and over-rated theatrical spectacle. There is no attempt to suggest the Rhine and the maidens do not swim, they are gymnasts on ropes. The gods and giants are dressed in East European uniformity and drabness and most of them are bald, including Erda. Nibelheim is all thick-pile carpet, Valhalla is a large square loudspeaker, the rainbow bridge is a coloured path across the stage and Fricka takes her vanity-case along.

On the other hand, Denby Richards in *Music and Musicians* (May 1978) had little but praise for the 'stunning' production and described Mills's Loge as 'the most convincing I have seen since Set Svanholm's great characterisation in the 1950s'. Gosh!

The second performance coincided with the first of two 1978 Congregations of Awards at which Companionship of the College – awarded for contribution of 'exceptional distinction' to the life and work of the College – was conferred on Dame Kathleen Ollerenshaw. Honorary Fellowships were conferred on the singers Dame Isobel Baillie and Sir Geraint Evans, the academics Professors Basil Deane and Friedrich Gürtler (Principal of the Royal Danish Academy of Music) and, from the RNCM staff, David Jordan, Joseph Ward and Percy Welton. At the Congregation of Awards in December 1978, the Honorary Fellows were two more singing Dames, Eva Turner and Janet Baker, Lady Barbirolli (who later donated her large private library of wind music to the College), the composer Peter Maxwell Davies, and Sydney Coulston, Anthony Hodges, the College librarian, and Gilbert Webster, senior tutor in percussion and for many years principal percussionist in the BBC Symphony Orchestra. It was because of his advice that the College possesses percussion equipment of the highest quality.

The joke went round that an exclusive club was to be formed for those who were *not* Honorary Fellows of the RNCM. There were other jokes too. Manduell liked to keep the choice of opera a state secret until the last possible moment, although he might indiscreetly 'leak' it to possible participants. This led John Rawnsley on one occasion to distribute a fake announcement that the next RNCM production was to be *The Desert Song*, with John Hanson in the leading role. (One member of staff confided to Rawnsley that she was delighted – it was her favourite operetta!) And there was the occasion when outsiders who had little or no connection with the College heard about its reasonably priced

Left to right: Robert Buning as Mime, Phillip Joll as Wotan and Keith Mills as Loge in the 1978 production of Wagner's Das Rheingold. Photograph: Sophie Baker

Christmas lunch in the refectory. A large queue formed. A student tenor, seeing members of the opera class far at the back of the queue, rolled to the floor with a cry of agony clutching his ample stomach and in his best operatic death-scene manner gasped: 'It's the Christmas pudding.' The gatecrashers melted away and the opera class were served in good time!

VI Warning Notes

At the 1978 awards ceremony, John Manduell reverted to his fears about the future of education in Britain and reported that immediate pressures may have lessened because there was 'some feeling abroad that education has paid its dues in meeting the general levy upon the nation'. But he sounded another warning about fees.

> Each student needs to find around £2,000 to meet his obligations in terms of fees and maintenance costs, and if a student does not qualify for a grant he can find himself in acute material difficulty ... Postgraduate and associate course students ... continue to be obliged to rely for support on a discretionary basis from local authorities which are increasingly hard-pressed and obliged to impose year by year ever more critical restrictions upon the amount of discretionary awards they can afford to make.

He cited a recent case of an RNCM student, 'a particularly hard-working and promising singer', who had abandoned her course because her local authority could not make her a discretionary grant. The graduands who received their diplomas from the Duchess on this occasion were the first to complete the RNCM four-year course.

It was at the end of March that the nation as a whole was made aware through television of the College's Concert Hall, for it was the venue for the semi-finals and finals of the BBC's first Young Musician of the Year competition. This aroused intense interest and controversy. There was a winner in each class – piano, strings, woodwind and brass – with £250 as the prize. Then the four winners competed in the final for £300 and a trophy. The age-limit was 19. The judges for the final, in which each contestant performed a concerto with the BBC Northern Symphony Orchestra conducted by Bryden Thomson, were Manduell (chairman), Yehudi Menuhin, Leon Goossens, Tamas Vasary, Harry Mortimer, Eleanor Warren, and David Ellis (then Head of Music, BBC North). They had to choose between the pianist Stephen Hough (the only RNCM finalist) playing Mozart, the cellist Caroline Dale playing Elgar, the clarinettist Michael Collins playing Finzi and the trombonist Michael Hext playing Gordon Jacob. To the amazement of the audience, who were equally divided on a 'straw vote' between Hough and Collins, the prize went to Hext. Among pianists eliminated in earlier

Congregation of Awards 1978: newly created Honorary Fellows of the College with the Duchess of Kent. Front row, left to right: Lady Barbirolli, Dame Eva Turner, Dame Janet Baker, Gilbert Webster. Back row: the College Librarian, Anthony Hodges, Peter Maxwell Davies and Sydney Coulston.

rounds was Barry Douglas, eventual outright winner of the Moscow Tchaikovsky Competition.

When the new academic year began in September, the School of Keyboard Studies had a new Head in Robert Elliott, who took over from Clifton Helliwell. Other retirements during the year were those of the soprano Ena Mitchell from the School of Vocal Studies and of Sheila Barlow, whose 'highly individual and invariably inspiring guidance' (Manduell's words) to opera students on the dramatic aspects of their work had covered over 30 years at the RMCM before she joined the RNCM staff. The College hosted the first Manchester International Organ Festival (won by John Scott, now organist and director of music at St Paul's Cathedral) from 2 to 8 September and in November the BBC's Young Composers' Forum was held at the College – 'without advertisement or adequate publicity and during half-term when most of the students were away', as Dominic Gill complained in the *Financial Times*. A better publicised event was the RNCM's own 'Schubertfest' from 17 to 22 November at which the 150th anniversary of Schubert's death was commemorated in six concerts which included song recitals by Thomas Hemsley and Alexander Young in addition to chamber music and two orchestral concerts conducted by Mark Elder and David Jordan.

Two Handel operas were chosen for the opera season from 30 November to 3 December. *Tamerlano* was performed by Musica nel Chiostro, conducted by Jane Glover and produced by Patrick Libby, with Alexander Young, Eiddwen Harrhy, Kevin Smith and Fiona Kimm in the cast. The College's contribution was a sumptuously designed (by Michael Holt) *Orlando*, produced by Brian Trowell and with Anne Dawson and Robin Martin-Oliver (later to marry) as Angelica and Orlando. In the *Musical Times* of February 1979, David Fallows wrote of this production's

> rich panoply of sets, its stylistically appropriate stage movement and its successful use of clouds and sudden changes such as are familiar from so many descriptions and engravings of 18th century opera … The greatest triumph was that of Anne Dawson, whose Angelica included unforgettable singing.

The College Symphony Orchestra, which earlier in the year had been conducted by Edward Downes, ended its 1978 season with Walter Susskind on the rostrum for Beethoven's First Symphony, Bartók's Concerto for Orchestra, and Franck's *Symphonic Variations* (solo pianist John Gough). During the year the

College had established its own chamber orchestra, with personnel entirely distinct from the Symphony Orchestra, under the conductorship of Michel Brandt.

In his report at the Congregation of Awards on 7 December 1978, Manduell allowed himself to dwell on College achievements: a library now containing over 30,000 books and scores, with a microfilm reader and a sound recording section; the winning of two composition prizes by David Gill and Paul Keenan; the award of the first Maggie Teyte singing prize to Deborah Rees, the Miriam Licette prize to Yvonne Lea, and the Leverhulme Prize at Glyndebourne to Jane Findlay; the double success of Christian Blackshaw in winning prizes at the Van Cliburn and Tchaikovsky competitions; and the winning of international prizes by strings and wind players from the College. In addition 14 singers received contracts from professional opera companies. There was also the encouraging success of Shirley Blakey's Junior Department, which had received a generous donation towards its work from the Siemens Foundation. With all this, the College was able to feel that others had more to learn from the Gulbenkian Foundation's report 'Training Musicians'. Its principal recommendation – that all colleges should run degree courses of a minimum four-year duration – had been RNCM policy from the first.

Cheerful news, such as the above, was needed at this date, for Britain was in the midst of the 'winter of discontent', when there were strikes in most of the public-sector services, dustbins were left unemptied and the dead unburied. Even so, College activities continued unabated, in spite of fuel cuts. In these conditions audiences heard a song recital by Sir Peter Pears, accompanied by the harpist Osian Ellis, and the six unaccompanied Cello Suites of J.S. Bach performed by Ralph Kirshbaum. The spring opera, from 26 March to 1 April, was Poulenc's *Les Dialogues des Carmélites*, produced by Timothy Tyrrel, conducted by David Jordan and with Vanessa Williamson, Jennifer Sharp, Yvonne Lea and Mark Curtis in the cast. But if singers seemed to enjoy much of the College limelight, there was compensation for instrumentalists in April when the RNCM's Brodsky Quartet won the Menuhin Prize at the Portsmouth International String Quartet Competition. These four students had revived the name of the famous quartet led for many years by Adolph Brodsky while he was Principal of the RMCM. This prize heralded their illustrious professional career. They had been playing together since school days. After the Portsmouth success, the Quartet won the contemporary music prize at Evian and toured Czechoslovakia and Jugoslavia under British Council auspices. There was critical

The RNCM Chamber Orchestra under its conductor Michel Brandt, performing in the Salle Varèse, Lyon, on its annual French tour. Photograph: Gérard Amsellem

Percy Welton, Head of Academic Studies 1980–89.

praise, too, for the group of RNCM students who gave the College's annual Wigmore Hall recital in July. A chance to compare standards had occurred in May when a string quartet from the Curtis Institute, Philadelphia, played at the College, followed a week later by a string trio from the Vienna Municipal High School for Music. In October there was a third exchange visit, from students of Freiburg's music school.

Nevertheless, opera continued to make the news. In May the College's production of *Orlando* was given two performances at the Bath Festival, with the Duchess of Kent attending the opening night in the Theatre Royal. Sir William Glock was the festival director; his previous attempt, a few years earlier, to take a college opera production into the festival had been frustrated by the Musicians' Union. This production had another two performances in November at the Maison de la Culture, Grenoble (the visit being wholly sponsored by the French authorities), preceded by one performance in Manchester. In July, Manduell announced a collaboration with Welsh National Opera whereby both would periodically share production costs when both had a common interest in wishing to mount a new production of the same opera.

In September 1979, the School of Theory and Humanities was re-named the School of Academic Studies (Percy Welton became Head in September 1980) and began major courses leading to the College's GMusRNCM award. This was probably the first degree-level work in a British conservatoire in which scholarship was the primary consideration with practical music-making playing an important but not dominant role. In this way, Manduell said,

> we have made important progress towards the objective to which we have firmly held since the inception of this College: the progressive elimination of the erstwhile dichotomy which artificially separated performance and academic study. Our firm policy is one of a fusion of these elements to the fullest extent which is realistic.

Familiar names recur throughout the programmes of RNCM events – regular piano recitals by Peter Donohoe, for example, and choral concerts by Stephen Wilkinson's William Byrd Singers. Walter Susskind returned to conduct the symphony and chamber orchestras. The July Chetham's concert at the RNCM ended in 1979 with Beethoven's Ninth Symphony in which the soloists were all RNCM staff or students: Jane Wunderley, Yvonne Lea, Alexander Young and Robert Dean. The RNCM Wind Ensemble's concert on 24 September had two conductors, Timothy Reynish and Sian Edwards, taking the first steps on her rapid rise to fame. She was at the RNCM from 1977 to 1981, entering as a horn-player to study with Ifor James, who had recommended the College to her. She became interested in conducting and, encouraged by Timothy Reynish, formed a wind octet. She was delighted to find that there was both the time and the physical space to put on internal concerts and she also took the octet to perform in Altrincham and at the Church of the Holy Name on Oxford Road, Manchester, and elsewhere. Looking back as the present music director of English National Opera on her RNCM days, she remembers how conscious she was of Manduell as the man who provided the impetus for the College's grand plans. 'When he was away, one was acutely aware that he was missing.'

The College also promoted two concerts in November 1979 to celebrate Sir Michael Tippett's forthcoming 75th birthday. On a foggy November evening, Paul Crossley played the first three piano sonatas, Robert Tear and Philip Ledger performed the song-cycle *Boyhood's End*, and the Lindsay Quartet played String Quartets Nos.1, 3 and 4. The College now had a contemporary music ensemble (which on 19 January 1980, conducted by David Drummond, gave the first British performance outside London of Henze's *Voices*), a baroque ensemble and the Big Band.

For the December opera the choice was Paisiello's *Il barbiere di Siviglia*, in its day a popular work but inevitably made redundant by Rossini's masterpiece. Yet it has much delightful and tuneful music. Malcolm Fraser produced the opera, David Jordan conducted and the cast was headed by Alison Barlow as Rosina, Anthony Jackman as Figaro and Mark Curtis as Almaviva. In May 1980 the production was taken to the Bath Festival. The Duchess of Kent attended a Manchester performance of the opera on the day she conferred Honorary Fellowships on Yehudi Menuhin, Myers Foggin and three staff members, Eleanor Warren, Timothy Reynish and Shirley Blakey. A new award was conferred for the first time, Honorary Membership of the College ('for persons who have given distinguished service to the College or whom the College wishes to honour for distinguished work in other spheres'). The first four Honorary Members were Alfred Alexander, the aural and laryngological surgeon, Brian Hill, clerk to the Council, Dr Samuel Oleesky, consultant physician, and Air Commodore Vaughan, the College Secretary.

John Pascoe's ingenious set for Paisiello's Il barbiere di Siviglia (1979) which toured to the Bath Festival in May 1980.

VII *Tightening the Belt*

Manduell's annual report in 1979 focused on the College's economies required by the national belt-tightening insisted upon by Mrs Thatcher's first Government after it had ousted Mr Callaghan's 'winter of discontent' Government at a general election. Further economies, he warned, could not be effected 'without causing marked damage to our fundamental work'. What the College now had in its sights was the construction of 'a substantial new building' to the west of the main RNCM building. This had been designed and was approved by all concerned. Its purpose was to accommodate the teaching overflow which for some time had been housed in Princess Building, an inconvenient distance from the College. This was due for demolition because of a new road system. (It was duly bulldozed in 1981, when the College secured a lease on St Ignatius School, a modern building not far from the College.) Nothing more was to happen about an extension until another 14 years had passed.

Students from Frankfurt's Municipal High School for Music performed at the College on 22 January 1980; and on 12 February annual exchanges with the Frankfurt School were initiated under British Council sponsorship by a concert by RNCM students in Frankfurt. This was followed by concerts in Saarbrücken and Wurzburg. On 26 February, in Manchester, students of Prague Academy performed music by Smetana, Dvořák, Martinů and some lesser-known Czech composers. The first result of the arrangement with Welsh National Opera was Dvořák's *The Jacobin*, which WNO was to perform in May. David Jordan conducted three RNCM performances in which Jennifer Sharp, Graham Macfarlan and Stephen Briggs sang the principal roles. Adrian Slack produced. Elizabeth Forbes, in the *Financial Times*, complained that three-quarters of Rodney Blumer's translation could not be heard because the orchestra drowned the singers. She blamed the conductor, whereas Stanley Sadie in *The Times* blamed Dvořák's over-generous scoring (the 1897 version was used in preference to the 1889 original). A fortnight later the second BBC Young Musician of the Year contest reached its climax when the finalists were Ronan O'Hora (piano), Clare McFarlane (violin), Nicholas Daniel (oboe) and Elaine Wolff (cornet). The winner was the oboist – a verdict that took 70 minutes to reach and was not unanimous.

An exciting feature of 1980 – extraordinarily daring when one remembers the financial climate at the time – was the formation of the RNCM Sinfonia, a full-time postgraduate chamber orchestra established under the aegis of the Faculty of Advanced Studies with financial aid from the Arts Council, the BBC (which guaranteed £20,000 a year for the first two years) and IBM (UK) Ltd. Its inaugural concert on 26 September was conducted by Michel Brandt. Bach's Suite No.3 in D was followed by Mozart's G major Violin Concerto (K216), in which the soloist was György Pauk, David Ellis's *Celebration*, written for the occasion, and Mozart's *Prague* Symphony. A major part in setting up this enterprise was played by Christopher Yates whose appointment from 1 September 1980 to the new post of Dean of Postgraduate Studies was announced in March. Yates, a Lancastrian born in Darwen in 1938, had been at the RMCM before taking a history degree at Cambridge. He reverted to music to study the flute with Geoffrey Gilbert at the Guildhall School of Music and Drama and from 1960 to 1965 was co-principal flautist in the Sadler's Wells Opera orchestra. He was personnel manager to the New Philharmonia Orchestra from 1965 until 1974, when he moved to Newcastle upon Tyne as general manager of the Northern Sinfonia. The RNCM's new Sinfonia, of 30 players, was planned to have an involvement with opera and a built-in tutorial system. Since the course lasted a year, this meant the personnel would change every year. The Sinfonia was formed against the wishes of several of the senior staff, who considered it a misconceived idea. But it was sustained for five years until Manduell allowed it to die, conceding the difficulty of obtaining enough good string players for each renewal.

Of other staff changes during the year, the retirement of John Wray as Dean of Studies takes priority. (The post was now divided into Dean of Undergraduate Studies, Terence Greaves, and the new Postgraduate appointment.) Dr Wray, a wise, genial and experienced musician, said his farewell by conducting Elgar's *The Dream of Gerontius* on 23 June. Maurice Clare, Colin Horsley and Charles Cracknell retired, as did Dorothy Pilling, Senior Tutor in Theoretical Studies.

Which other college, one wonders, would have marked, as the RNCM did on 3 November, the centenary of the composer J.H. Foulds? He had been a cellist in Richter's Hallé and later composed incidental music for Shaw's *St Joan* and a *World Requiem* (in 1923) which for a time had a vogue. But his music had been neglected for decades and was due for revival. Five of his works, a string quartet, a song-cycle, the cello sonata and two piano pieces, were performed by Meriel Dickinson (mezzo-soprano), Moray Welsh (cello), Ronald Stevenson (piano) and the Endellion Quartet.

The College's first Mozart opera was staged on three evenings in December when Michel Brandt conducted *Così fan tutte* with the RNCM Sinfonia in the pit.

Christopher Yates, appointed Dean of Postgraduate Studies in 1980. Photograph: Hanya Chlala

Malcolm Fraser produced it elegantly and economically, with designs by Fay Conway which had been used earlier in the summer for Berlioz's *Beatrice and Benedict* at the Buxton Festival. The undoubted star of the performance was Anne Dawson as Fiordiligi. The Dorabella was Deborah Stuart-Roberts and Despina was sung by Joan Rodgers. The power of Mozart's music to move the soul was a theme of what the Duchess of Kent – and she is not alone – considers to have been one of the most affecting events in the College's history when Lord Boyle, the Vice-Chancellor of Leeds University, a former Minister of Education, and chairman of the Leeds Piano Competition juries, spoke on behalf of the honorary graduands at the Congregation of Awards on 11 December. In reference to the education cuts, he said:

> I hope no one in this audience this afternoon will fail, as Churchill would have said, to fight his corner when it comes to the battle to secure adequate prospects for those who have been trained at this College. I would just add this – yes, certainly there is a growing place in the arts for private sponsorship. That, I hope and believe, has come to stay. But there is also no substitute for adequate public levels of support on the part both of central and local government.

Then, in a passage made more poignant for his listeners because he was so obviously a dying man, he said:

> Sadly, for purely physical reasons over which I have no control, my own involvement in the world of music will now have to become more limited, though I do not intend that it should cease altogether … I do wonder whether anyone outside the world of professional music can ever have loved this art more than I have done. And when I listened recently to the new Karajan recording of *The Magic Flute*, when I listened to the second side of the first act, from the March of the Priests to the end of Sarastro's second aria, I felt a quite renewed and special sense of the beauty of the sound, of the implied dimension, even in a recording, of operatic spectacle and a conviction that here is composition which represents the human imagination at its highest possible stretch, and I felt that to have known and loved music of this transcendent quality has of itself, quite apart from anything else, made life seem to have been infinitely worth living.

Lord Boyle was made an Honorary Member in company with John Boyce, former chief education officer of Lancashire County Council, John Bower, RNCM recording manager, John Tomlinson, Cheshire County Council education director,

and Ursula Vaughan Williams. The Honorary Fellows were headed by Plácido
Domingo, with the composers Alun Hoddinott and Alexander Goehr, the
conductor Edward Downes, and Michel Brandt, Robert Elliott, and Geoffrey
Jackson from the College staff. An opera-rehearsal incident involving Downes has
become a College legend. The temperamental leading soprano, continually
upbraided by the conductor for not watching him and thus getting a bar behind,
burst into tears and pointed to the tenor, crying: 'You're always picking on me.
Why don't you pick on him?' 'Never mind him,' Downes replied. 'He's four bars
behind.'

A happy beginning to 1981 was the appointment as OBE of the piano tutor
Gordon Green who, alas, did not live long to enjoy the honour. The catalogue of
awards to students was lengthened on 4 February when the brother and sister
Michael and Jacqueline Thomas, members of the Brodsky Quartet, won the first
Concerto Award, sponsored by Bass Northwest, for their playing of Brahms's
Double Concerto for violin and cello. And on 27 February the Students' Union
promoted its first opera, a semi-staged performance in the Concert Hall of
Mozart's *Don Giovanni* conducted by Sian Edwards. A former student, Henry
Herford, returned to sing the title-role, Barry Banks sang Ottavio, Gidon Saks the
Commendatore, and Zerlina, to quote Paul Dewhirst in the *Daily Telegraph*, 'was
the charming Linda Kitchen ... We shall hear more of her, I fancy.' He was right.
The next operatic event, attended by the Duchess, was the world première of the
College's first full-length opera commission, Alun Hoddinott's *The Trumpet
Major*, adapted from Hardy's novel by Myfanwy Piper. Few of the critics liked
the music much. 'This was not a happy commission for the RNCM who
nevertheless present the work with great enthusiasm,' Paul Griffiths wrote in *The
Times*. Everybody liked Robin Don's beautiful sets and Basil Coleman's
production was admired, along with the singing of Zena Jones, Philip Creesy and
Jeremy Munro. The conductor was David Jordan. The following week the RNCM
gave two performances of the opera in the New Theatre, Cardiff, as guests of
Welsh National Opera.

Opera was the talk of Mancunian cultural life at this time. In the late 1970s
both the city's major commercial theatres, the Opera House and the Palace, had
been closed, depriving the touring opera companies of a home. But in 1979 a
music-loving Manchester businessman, Raymond Slater, formed a trust and
bought the Palace. The theatre was refurbished and its stage enlarged so that
Covent Garden productions could easily be accommodated there. The
impression was given by the Royal Opera that it would make the Palace its

*11 December 1980 - at the reception for the Congregation
of Awards. Left to right: Ursula Vaughan Williams
(Honorary Member), Plácido Domingo (Honorary Fellow),
Joseph Ward (then Assistant Head of Vocal Studies) and
Alexander Young (then Head of Vocal Studies).*

Bellini's La Sonnambula, 1981. Left to right: Anne Dawson as Amina, Anthony Mee as Elvino and Gwion Thomas as the Notary.

second home, with visits by the opera and ballet in alternate years. The opera came twice and the ballet once. English National Opera undertook one visit. But the London companies then abandoned touring and only Opera North and Glyndebourne Touring Opera regularly visited the Palace Theatre. Eventually the theatre was sold again to a commercial company and has reverted to its traditional role as a home for musicals: a sad story, though this is not the place to tell it in full. But in May 1981 euphoria prevailed and for the Royal Opera's first visit that month, the RNCM arranged a series of talks on the operas to be performed (*Otello, Lohengrin, Tosca* and *Die Zauberflöte*), by Harold Rosenthal, Gerhard Hüsch, and Dame Eva Turner, among others.

The College had undertaken a tour of its own when the RNCM Sinfonia visited the Evian-les-Bains Festival in early May. This festival's theme was youth – its programmes were played by youth orchestras from various countries and there was a competition for string quartets at which the Brodsky won the award already chronicled. Under Michel Brandt, the Sinfonia, in its three concerts, played Mozart, Haydn and Ravel and also Maxwell Davies's *Sinfonia*. The concerts were given in the town's casino. This was the first of several regular visits to Europe each summer by the Sinfonia.

Critical comment on the Sinfonia's performances in its first year tended to be muted and Manduell, in his report on 1981, began to have doubts as he wondered

> whether the scheme is in current conditions as important to string players as to their counterparts in the woodwind and brass sections. The continuing (if diminishing) shortage of good string players nationally still encourages talented young graduates to proceed direct to first appointment, so forswearing the opportunity to consolidate their skills by postgraduate study. The longer-term viability of this new course in postgraduate orchestral studies must therefore be assessed in these terms and be measured by the degree of effectively balanced recruitment which proves possible over the next year or two.

In another year of student successes in various international competitions, pride of place should go to the College's first victory in the Kathleen Ferrier Memorial Scholarship. This was awarded in May to Joan Rodgers, a third-year student with Joseph Ward. She had entered the College as a mezzo-soprano (having already achieved a Liverpool University degree in foreign languages, including Russian), but had become a soprano (and sang *Caro nome* from *Rigoletto* in the Ferrier competition). She used the £2,000 prize money to finance a fourth year at the College. She is now one of Britain's leading singers. She had intended to spend one or at the most two years at the College.

> Somehow (she says) two years turned into four of the happiest and most constructive years of my life. The College has one of those atmospheres totally conducive to good work. There is such a buzz of energy and enthusiasm, which always makes our job easier. Probably that has much to do with its being an arts centre as well as an educational establishment. One always felt at the heart of the performing world there. There was an abundance of opportunities to hear some of the world's best performers. There can be no better preparation for any student wishing to make a career as a performer than being immersed in live music.

Miss Rodgers's success in the Ferrier prize was emulated in 1982 by Anne Dawson and in 1983 by Louise Jackson. A great soprano of an earlier age, Eva Turner, gave in 1981 a major part of her personal library to the RNCM. The College library was also the recipient of a complete set of all publications under the imprint of the Scandinavian music publisher Wilhelm Hansen & Co and its subsidiaries. American interests sponsored the first international conference of symphonic wind bands in July, when the College was host to over 1,000 young wind players from all over the world, a tribute to the proselytizing energy of Tim Reynish who, a few months later, went to the United States on a Churchill Trust travelling fellowship to visit leading American universities and music colleges and study the wind-band repertory there.

The December opera production was of Bellini's *La Sonnambula*, with Anne Dawson as Amina, Andrea Bolton as Lisa and a promising second-year tenor, Anthony Mee, as Elvino. The production was another Malcolm Fraser-Fay Conway confection – 'Swiss chocolate box', said Paul Dewhirst. The Duchess's attendance at a performance coincided as usual with the Congregation of Awards when the new Honorary Members included Sir Bernard Lovell of Jodrell Bank, Sir Denis Forman of Granada, John Vallins of Chetham's School, and Keith Murgatroyd, the College's design consultant. The new Fellows included Sir William Glock, David Lumsden, Principal of the Royal Academy of Music, and, from the College staff, Betty Bannerman, Anthony Gilbert and Brian Hughes. Betty Bannerman was among staff members who retired in 1981. Others were John Hoffman, the keyboard technician, Patrick Ireland, Clifford Knowles, Audrey Langford, Irene Wilde and Maimie Woods. The ranks of those who had served the old colleges as well as the new were thinning.

Anthony Gilbert, Senior Tutor in Composition. Photograph: Hanya Chlala

VIII *Ordeal by Cuts*

*Joan Rodgers as Pamina and Ian Platt as Papageno in the 1982
production of Mozart's Die Zauberflöte*

The appointment as CBE of John Manduell in the New Year Honours began 1982 on a bright note. He had in 1980 been the first recipient of the Leslie Boosey Award for services to contemporary music, acknowledgement not only of his work at the RNCM but of his achievements since 1969 as programme director of the Cheltenham Festival. In July came the news that in the Tchaikovsky piano competition in Moscow, Peter Donohoe had been awarded joint second prize with Vladimir Ovchinikov, the first prize being withheld.

Sian Edwards's name appeared regularly as conductor of one or other of the College's orchestras and the pianist Peter Seivewright was another admired student performer. For the February opera season, Walton's *The Bear* was revived to mark the composer's 80th birthday in a new production by Thomas Hemsley, with Deborah Stuart-Roberts and Keith Latham. It shared a double bill with Bartók's *Bluebeard's Castle*, in which a Swedish student, Margaretha Orvelius, and Stephen Richardson sang Judith and Bluebeard. This was followed in March by five performances of Mozart's *Die Zauberflöte*. Joan Rodgers's singing of Pamina won her ecstatic press notices and resulted in the start of her professional career in the same role at the Aix Festival that summer. There was high praise for Barry Banks's Tamino, Stephen Richardson's Sarastro, Linda Kitchen's Papagena, Evelyn Nicholson's Queen of Night and for the Three Ladies – Jane Eaglen, Elizabeth Gaskell and Yvonne Howard – whom I described at the time (not inaccurately) as 'Valkyries in the making'.

These bright events were needed, for in the first quarter of the year the RNCM entered its worst financial crisis as a result of the Government's deep cuts into the higher education programme. The College was hit hard because, along with the Birmingham School of Music and unlike the London colleges, it was funded from the Department of Education and Science's advanced further education pool. A substantial and unpredicted supplementary cut, amounting to 33 per cent, was inflicted. Despite their own difficulties, the four local authorities agreed to compensate two-thirds of this shortfall. Even so the College had to reduce its revenue expenditure by £250,000. This meant a reduction in staff through a voluntary early-retirement scheme. 'We are reaching,' Manduell said, 'or may even have already reached, the point at which we can no longer provide courses of the range and quality which it is our proper responsibility to offer.'

Retirements, therefore, were more numerous than usual (they included Rudolf Botta). In October the College's first secretary, 'Manny' Vaughan, retired too – 'invigorating, imaginative and tireless endeavours on our behalf' and 'as fine a serving officer as any institution could expect or hope to know' were words of praise from Manduell no more effusive than the recipient deserved. He was succeeded by Frank Mais, a former senior civil servant.

Frank Mais, College Secretary 1982–1990.

The strength of the cello school in the College at this time was reflected when Elizabeth Anderson performed Shostakovich's first concerto with the RNCM Chamber Orchestra and Mark Sheridan played Walton's concerto with the Symphony Orchestra. A new name among the singers which is now familiar to opera-goers was that of John Connell, who sang Polyphemus in a concert performance of Handel's *Acis and Galatea,* with the Baroque Ensemble under David Francis. The year's final opera production, conducted by Edward Downes, was of Verdi's *Ernani*, the second joint venture with WNO. Evelyn Nicholson sang Elvira, Anthony Mee was Ernani and Keith Latham sang Don Carlo. The Duchess attended the performance on 9 December, having earlier admitted Francis Jackson, Organist of York Minster, Dr Hans-Dieter Resch, Rektor of the Frankfurt Hochschule für Musik, and three members of the staff, Christopher Yates, John Cameron, and the trombone tutor (and former Hallé principal) Terence Nagle to Honorary Fellowship. A firm friend of the College, Lord Rhodes of Saddleworth, was made an Honorary Member in company with Sir William Downward, Lord Lieutenant of Greater Manchester, Albert Hague, a former member of the NSM Council as well as that of the RNCM, and Sidney Palmer, the bursar. With Henry Herford winning the International American Competition for singers and Stephen Hough taking the first Terence Judd award for pianists (in 1983 he also won the Naumberg Foundation Award in Carnegie Hall, New York) the Duchess's attendance at the College's Christmas Ball set the seal on a year when Lord Boyle's injunction to 'fight your corner' had soon been put to the test.

The College reached its tenth anniversary in 1983 and in April launched an appeal for funds. The RNCM, Manduell pointed out, had been 'seriously impoverished' by four years of cuts in central government funding. Had it not been for the four constituent local authorities, the College might have had to close. The appeal, he said, was to provide or restore the icing on the cake. Did they need cake and icing?

Bread alone will not enable us to help students to reach the heights of excellence ... If those who study here are to enjoy inspiration and opportunity comparable to that to be found at, say, the Juilliard School … then the concentration of resources needed (so much in music has to be individually taught) must be of an appropriate order. We recognise that these are necessarily times of constraint and restraint and we do not press for the ale; but the cake is essential and the alternative is unquestionably mediocrity.

The 'icing' the appeal was intended to restore comprised guest conductors, master classes, assistance in buying an instrument, library acquisitions, endowment funds for the Junior School, and much else. As if to emphasise the positive, the Council approved the introduction of Junior Fellowships in the Faculty of Advanced Studies for 1983-4. And the recording department produced a two-LP album reviewing in words and music the first ten years of the College.

The launch of the appeal was marked by a service in Manchester Cathedral on 12 June, attended by the Duke of Kent in the absence through illness of his wife, and by a gala concert that evening in the Opera Theatre at which Brian Redhead was master of ceremonies. The conducting was shared between James Loughran, David Jordan and Brian Hughes and the past and present College students who gave their services were Peter Donohoe, who had flown from Leningrad where he had played the same concerto, Rachmaninov's C minor, the previous evening, Joan Rodgers in Mozart and Lehár, John Rawnsley in *Eri tu* from Verdi's *Un ballo in maschera*, and Jane Eaglen as Aida in the *finale* of Act II. Yet perhaps the anniversary event which many will recall with acute pleasure was the midsummer banquet on 24 June, attended by the Duchess, held on a glorious evening in multi-coloured marquees in the garden of Hartley Hall. To quote the annual report:

> Within, the vivid floral decorations, mellowed by the gentle glow of candlelight as the evening progressed, provided an agreeable Mancunian form of Athenian backdrop for the presentation from Britten's *A Midsummer Night's Dream* which ended the evening.

Next day the Duchess toured the College, visiting the students' union, library and recording department and, in the evening, presenting the Bass Concerto Award to the pianist Ronan O'Hora, who played Beethoven's G major concerto, conducted by Sir Charles Groves.

In what would have been the year of Britten's 70th birthday, the College staged two of his operas. In March, Yvonne Howard sang Lucretia in *The Rape of Lucretia*, with Nicholas Buxton and Deborah Stuart-Roberts as the Male and

The Duchess of Kent tours the Library during a Summer visit to the College in 1984.

Female Chorus, Gwion Thomas as Tarquinius and Clive Bayley as Collatinus. Jordan conducted and the production was by Malcolm Fraser, one of those in which his propensity for relating everything, however unlikely, to the threat of nuclear war was particularly marked. Lucretia was shown as some kind of martyr of Greenham Common, the American air base in Buckinghamshire outside which a camp of militantly anti-nuclear women took up residence for months. In November the choice, a bold one, was the neglected *Gloriana*, finely conducted by Anthony Hose, well designed by Deirdre Clancy and elegantly produced by David Penn. Elizabeth I was sung impressively, indeed regally, by Deborah Stuart-Roberts, with Nicholas Buxton as Essex and John Connell as the blind Ballad Singer again making his mark, as he had done earlier in the year in a performance of Brahms's *Requiem* conducted by Timothy Reynish.

Deborah Stuart-Roberts as Queen Elizabeth and Gwion Thomas as Sir Robert Cecil in the 1983 production of Britten's Gloriana.

Space precludes a survey of all the music played in the College this and any other year, but just to read through the brochures is to be reminded of memorable evenings, whether it be Donohoe in Prokofiev, a young and conventionally dressed Nigel Kennedy playing Mendelssohn's concerto with the RNCM Sinfonia, an outstanding performance of Schoenberg's Piano Concerto by Kathryn Turner, with Reynish conducting, a piano recital by Vovka Ashkenazy (son of Vladimir) who was completing his last year at the College as a pupil of Sulamita Aronovsky, or Paul Almond's playing of Shostakovich's Second Violin Concerto. And a famous former RMCM student returned on 7 October to give a recital in aid of the Appeal – John Ogdon played Beethoven, Schumann (*Carnaval*) and Liszt. Among those who gave recitals to help the Appeal were the guitarist John Williams, the flautist James Galway, the violinist Lydia Mordkovich and the cellist Ralph Kirshbaum.

When the Duchess made her annual visit to present awards, she spoke of her pride in a decade of achievement. 'I want you to know how much I treasure the honour of being your president.' She conferred Companionship of the College on Sir Charles Groves, the chairman of the Council. The first former RNCM students to have Honorary Fellowship conferred on them were Peter Donohoe and John Rawnsley, alongside the guitarists Julian Bream and John Williams, and David Ellis of the BBC. The Honorary Members were Raymond Slater, Raphael Gonley, who was then Director of North West Arts and a member of the Council, Richard Godlee, deputy chairman of the Hallé Concerts Society, and David Andrews, Warden of Hartley Hall.

Financially the College now had to contend with a National Advisory Body, set up by the Government to take responsibility for the rest of higher education in England and Wales comparable with that exercised by the University Grants Committee and, it was hoped, to rationalise the distribution of the restricted resources available. The NAB's first 'report' on the RNCM was encouraging and meant that no further reductions in expenditure were necessary. No further progress was made on the extension building and the lease on St Ignatius expired during 1984 without option for renewal. In its place the College leased the former North West Science Museum building in Grosvenor Street.

Continually the College was trying to make improvements. An overhaul of catering occurred, with Martin Angell appointed manager in January 1984, and computerisation was further developed. As far as teaching was concerned, advantage was taken of the enthusiasm for 'early music' and there were now classes in various period instruments – cornett, sackbut, baroque flute, baroque strings and viols, with specialist visiting tutors in all these disciplines.

A blow, however, was the Arts Council's decision to withdraw its financial support from the RNCM Sinfonia. Since its inception four years earlier, and after a nervous start, the Sinfonia had fulfilled its purpose of giving graduates a concentrated year in which to refine their skills. Of the 109 students who had played in the orchestra in that time, 80 had subsequently secured posts in professional orchestras. Each summer the Sinfonia had visited France, in 1983 giving 15 concerts in 19 days.

Eleanor Warren, Head of the School of Strings, retired at the end of the 1984 summer term. Tutors on her staff and former students performed Strauss's *Metamorphosen* as a farewell tribute to a remarkable woman who had raised the School's standard to a peak. She was succeeded by Rodney Slatford, the double bass player. Terence Greaves was about to become Acting Principal for 15 months while Manduell had 'grace leave' as director of the British contribution to European Music Year. Several students from the European Community were at the College in addition to those from Australia, Austria, China, Hong Kong, Hungary, South Africa, the United States and Zimbabwe.

The College was by now accustomed to competition successes by its singers and instrumentalists but its first conducting success was registered on 14 May

Rodney Slatford, appointed Head of Strings in 1984.
Photograph: Hanya Chlala

1984 when Sian Edwards, youngest of the three finalists, won the first Leeds Conductors' Competition. Various awards went to singers, nevertheless – Louise Winter, Deborah Stuart-Roberts, Anne Williams-King, John Connell and Gwion Thomas – and Rachel Brown, a flautist, won the young artist's competition of the National Flute Association of America. Not to be outdone, the pianists William Fong and Julian Evans won competitions.

Having earlier produced Paisiello's *Il barbiere di Siviglia*, Malcolm Fraser, in April 1984, ingeniously adapted the sets from that staging for his production of Rossini's masterpiece on the same subject. David Jordan conducted three performances and Gareth Jones two. There were two casts, only Ian Platt as Dr Bartolo and Claire Daniels as Berta singing in both. Almaviva was shared by Barry Banks and Paul Nilon, Figaro by Mark Holland and Gwion Thomas, Basilio by John Connell and Clive Bayley and Rosina by Meinir Williams and Andrea Bolton. The opera was also performed at the Theatr Clwyd, Mold. A few weeks later the College was reminded that it was not alone in its adventurously high standards when the Leicestershire Schools Symphony Orchestra performed a programme containing first performances of works by Rupert Bawden and Douglas Young, Elliott Carter's *Pocahontas* and Dallapiccola's *Symphonic Fragments (Marsia)*.

This orchestra had been a special interest of Sir Michael Tippett, who was one of the 1984 Honorary Fellows just over three weeks before his 80th birthday. He was honoured in company with Sir Peter Pears, and, from the College staff, the singing teacher Caroline Crawshaw (two of whose students had won the Ferrier Scholarship) and the piano tutor Derrick Wyndham, teacher of Peter Donohoe among others. The Honorary Members were James Anderton, Chief Constable of Greater Manchester, the Earl of Harewood, former President of the RMCM, Brian Redhead and – a thoughtful award – Mrs Helen Trueman, the College's senior telephonist, 'who for eleven years has daily offered to every caller a friendly and helpful reception'. There being no winter opera, the Duchess attended a concert at which Sian Edwards conducted Tippett's Fourth Symphony, in the composer's presence, and Elgar's *Enigma Variations*.

Others of the College's prizewinners rightly gave recitals – Julian Evans after winning the Dudley piano competition and Julie Price, the bassoonist who won the 1985 Bass Concerto award – but there were also in the early months of 1985 concerts by the College's percussion ensemble, performing new works, and by the College's composers – Simon Parkin, Priti Paintal, Malcolm Scott, Alison Cox and Brian Hughes.

(above) Mark Tinkler as the eponymous hero (centre) in the 1984 production of Britten's Billy Budd.
(left) Michael Holt's magnificent set for the production.

On 16 March, David Lloyd-Jones, then music director of Opera North, conducted the first three performances (Simon Phipps conducted a fourth) of Britten's *Billy Budd*, produced by Joseph Ward, who had sung Billy under the composer's direction in 1960, and designed (superbly) by Michael Holt. The *Daily Telegraph*'s critic declared that all previous College achievements had been surpassed in 'a production which confronts head-on and overcomes the challenges of Britten's great opera. Musically, emotionally and dramatically, this was a triumphant occasion.' He gave high praise to Mark Tinkler's Billy, Clive Bayley's Claggart and Geraint Dodd's Captain Vere, 'and throughout there is the superb chorus almost unbearably moving in the "Hilo" chorus … ' (On the last night, with Billy just about to be hanged, a fire alarm rang and within seconds the ship's company of *HMS Indomitable* was in the street outside the College. A fire in the kitchens was extinguished and the performance was resumed after half an hour.)

Joseph Ward dedicated the first night to the memory of Frederic Cox, former Principal of the RMCM and teacher of many talented singers to emerge from both the RMCM and RNCM. He had died on 2 March. In his memory, an annual singing prize, the Frederic Cox Award for senior students, was established at the College, funded by the Ralph Vaughan Williams Trust. A performance of Verdi's *Requiem* was given in the Opera Theatre in memory of this admired and much-loved man on 11 January 1986 at which the soloists were his former pupils Rosalind Plowright (who flew in from Frankfurt specially for the performance), Sandra Browne, Arthur Davies and Gwynne Howell. Timothy Reynish conducted and the performance was prefaced by a tribute by Lord Harewood, who had been President of the RMCM throughout Cox's years as Principal.

But back to 1985, which was the tercentenary of the births of J.S. Bach, Handel and Domenico Scarlatti. The College's second spring opera production was therefore Handel's *Teseo*, conducted by Stephen Cleobury with an all-female cast – only its second public performance since 1713. Malcolm Fraser's production, designed by Lez Brotherston, set the work in a stately home being used for First World War wounded, with gas-masked men as the powers of darkness. Hilary Finch in *The Times* found it less trying than some others and praised the singing of Diana Palmer, Louise Jackson, Gillian Webster and Janice Close. (Incidentally, for some years now the College had established the pleasant custom of serving pre-opera dinners in the Senior Common Room.)

Terence Greaves had a busy and eventful year to report. Even by RNCM expectations, the prizewinners did well. The baritone Simon Keenlyside won the Pears competition with Jeremy Fisher winning the accompanists' prize. The singer Jane Findlay won the Miriam Licette Scholarship for study abroad. Ronan O'Hora won the Stefania Niekrasz piano prize. Julie Price, bassoonist, was awarded the Worshipful Company of Musicians' Medal. Andrew Wilde, a Bakst pupil, won the Dudley piano competition and a week later the LPO-Pioneer Young Soloist of the Year award. In a recent Glyndebourne Touring Opera production of Britten's *A Midsummer Night's Dream*, Greaves was able to boast, eight of the principals were ex-RNCM, with six former and four current College students in the chorus. In addition, Peter Donohoe established a prize in his

Clark Rundell with the RNCM Big Band.
Photograph: Gerry Murray

name and on 4 November gave a recital of Tippett, Beethoven and Chopin to establish it. John Ogdon returned on 3 December to give the first performance of his *Kaleidoscope* and to play works by McCabe, Ellis, Pitfield, Elliott and Stevenson in aid of a scholarship in memory of Gordon Green.

In September 1985, for the first time, 500 students were enrolled at the College. It had taken 12 years to reach this optimum figure, principally because only students with the necessary general educational qualifications had been accepted. Elitism was not, and never should be, a dirty word at the RNCM. But the College was now at a disadvantage because it was the only major conservatoire without designation by the Department of Education and Science for the Professional Performance course. It was frustrating, Greaves pointed out, that talented students who wanted to enter the RNCM had to accept places elsewhere to qualify for a mandatory award. The financial outlook was gloomy all round, but money had been found to improve access to the College for the disabled and also to improve the tutorial rooms' heating and ventilation – yet again! The Concert Hall organ was refurbished, new pianos were bought, and the College furthered its reputation as the national centre for wind-band music and again hosted the British Association of Symphonic Bands and Wind Ensembles' conference. Here the entrepreneurial skills of Timothy Reynish were strengthened by the advent of the engaging American postgraduate Junior Fellow in Conducting, Clark Rundell. As always, the library and recording departments improved their already noteworthy services. Visiting soloists were always surprised to be given a recording of their performance within minutes of its ending.

There was opera again for the Duchess in 1985 after she had conferred Honorary Fellowships on Eli Goren, recently retired from the School of Strings, and John Hosier, then Principal of the Guildhall School of Music and Drama, and conferred Honorary Membership on Sir John Tooley, general director of the Royal Opera, Clive Smart, general manager of the Hallé, and Peter Moores, a philanthropist whose generosity to opera and singers seems boundless. The opera was Debussy's *Pelléas et Mélisande*, produced and designed by Malcolm Fraser – his last College opera production before he left for Cincinnati – and conducted by David Jordan at the first of three performances and then by Sir Charles Groves. Gwion Thomas and Meinir Williams sang the title-roles, with Mark Glanville as Golaud. Suffice it to say that this evocative production, well sung and magnificently played, was all that RNCM standards had led audiences to expect.

x *Centres of Excellence*

John Manduell took up the reins again in 1986 and at once found himself embroiled in a tricky controversy. Sir David Lumsden, Principal of the Royal Academy of Music, had caused a stir by announcing that, in a bid to improve its funding, the Academy proposed to become a 'centre of excellence', with superstar teachers. Nothing wrong with that, it was the RAM's right and prerogative. However, the Secretary of State for Education and Science, Sir Keith Joseph – spurred, it was rumoured, by some disappointment experienced by a music-student relative – unwisely allied himself with the Academy's ambitions and bemoaned the fact that Britain's music colleges did not produce first-class international soloists. There was a hint that the DES might designate the Academy as *the* music college, and that there would be no more money overall, but the Academy might enjoy a privileged funding position. Obviously this possibility, whether seriously intended or not, united the other music colleges in protest. After much wordy debate in the press, the matter died when Sir Keith was replaced in a Cabinet re-shuffle.

Manduell was at pains to insist that there was no battle between the RAM and the other colleges. But, he explained

> it may be permissible to express regret that attempts to secure from the DES more realistic provision for music colleges were not undertaken by all the music colleges collaborating closely in the way pursued by the universities rather than by separate initiatives, as has occurred.

Happily, the Academy resumed full participation in the work of the Committee of Music Colleges. That Britain was 'losing out' in the soloist stakes was, Manduell considered, a questionable thesis.

> Even if it be true that we have not done as well as some other countries in producing internationally recognised soloists in certain disciplines (for example, violinists), we have more than compensated for this in others (for instance, singers and pianists). These matters depend in any event upon so many factors beyond the control of a minister or a music college …

Mozart's *Idomeneo* was the spring opera, with five performances conducted by Wilfried Boettcher, with the RNCM Chamber Orchestra in the pit, and produced by Peter Ebert. The sets by John and Margaret Sheard vividly re-created the Palace of Knossos. Geraint Dodd, later to be first recipient of the Webster Booth Esso Award, sang Idomeneo, with Jane Carpenter as Elettra, Paul Trotter as Idamante and the role of Ilia sung at different performances by Janice Close and Gillian Webster. This was the last opera to be performed under the aegis of Alexander Young as Head of the School of Vocal Studies. He retired in the summer, the last of the original Heads of Schools to go. Manduell's tribute to 'Basil' was more than just a statutory encomium. 'There has been no better loved member of our staff … There is no one in the College who did not regret his retirement.' Unobtrusively but firmly, Young insisted upon and maintained the highest standards, as results proved. He was succeeded by Joseph Ward, with Christopher Underwood as Assistant Head. In Young's last year, Simon Keenlyside won the first Frederic Cox Award and the Richard Tauber Memorial Prize, Ida-Maria Turri won the Maggie Teyte Prize and the Eva Turner Bursary, Janice Close won the Kathleen Ferrier Memorial Scholarship and the John Christie Award at Glyndebourne, and Gillian Webster won Scottish Opera's John Noble Prize.

It was also a successful year for composers, with Harrison Birtwistle and Simon Bainbridge as Visiting Tutors during Anthony Gilbert's sabbatical leave in Australia. A former student, Simon Holt, was composer-in-residence at the Bath Festival and was performed at a Tokyo festival. Martin Butler had commissions from Crete and Australia, Keith Gifford won the City of Trieste prize with an orchestral work and there was good news of both Alison Cox and Priti Paintal. Recent new members of staff included the pianist Denis Matthews, the clarinettist Alan Hacker and, as Supervisor in Chamber Music, Christopher Rowland, formerly of the Fitzwilliam String Quartet.

In 1986 the College and the Royal Scottish Academy of Music and Drama became full and equal partners in the Associated Board of the Royal Schools of Music. It was also the year in which Dame Kathleen Ollerenshaw retired from chairmanship of the Court. The College has never had a better friend nor a more whole-hearted advocate and champion, healthily impatient of any opposition. To watch her chairing a difficult meeting was an object lesson in the true art of politics. Knowing local government inside out and being able to spot at a moment's notice who among councillors was likely to make most trouble, she deployed all her wiles, which did not exclude feminine charm, to cajole and eventually outwit any source of danger. She knew when to listen and when to bring her deafness, of which many were unaware, to her (and the College's) aid.

Sir Harrison Birtwistle (right), Visiting Tutor in Composition, gives a master class. Photograph: Camera Five Four

She was indefatigable. Her retirement was marked by a convivial dinner on the stage of the Opera Theatre. She was succeeded by Professor Stanley Henig, of Lancaster, a devoted and knowledgeable opera enthusiast.

Much is written here of the achievements of students, but those of the staff should not be overlooked. Many of the instrumental teachers also pursued successful careers on the concert-platform; and Dr Douglas Jarman, Tutor in Historical, Theoretical and Aural Studies, was a world authority on the music of Alban Berg and Kurt Weill. He was among the new Honorary Fellows on 10 December, in company with John McCabe, Patrick McGuigan and John Ogdon. The Honorary Members were Sir George Christie of Glyndebourne, Sir John Burgh of the British Council and James Maxwell of the Royal Exchange Theatre.

XI *Corporate Status*

Sally Harrison in the title role of Massenet's Manon, *1987.*
Photograph: Gerry Murray

In 1987 there was an intensification of the College's exchanges with foreign conservatoires. Students from Frankfurt, Belgrade, Lyon and Oslo visited Manchester. College representatives visited Austria, Germany, Jugoslavia and Hong Kong, orchestras and ensembles toured to the Channel Islands, Scotland and Switzerland in addition to giving many performances in English towns and festivals. The RNCM Chamber Orchestra again visited France where it was now virtually the resident orchestra of the Aix Festival. This pattern has been maintained to the present day and is now taken for granted as part of the College's routine and *raison d'être*.

Rodney Slatford's innovative enthusiasm as Head of the School of Strings was responsible for weekends in 1986 and 1987 when string-playing children were invited into the College to be coached by musicians such as Emmanuel Hurwitz, Sheila Nelson, Richard Deakin, Malcolm Layfield and Cynthia Yates. This was followed by Violin Day, Brass Day, Reed-making Day and other 'Days'. At a 'Double Reed Festival' an orchestra of over 60 oboes and 50 bassoons, drawn from throughout Britain, performed Handel's *Fireworks Music* in the Opera Theatre. Nor was this all. One of the great jazz saxophonists, Don Rendell, worked with the Big Band, itself a virtuoso ensemble, and the brass ensembles flourished under Clark Rundell, Howard Snell and Tim Reynish. Maxim Shostakovich visited the College to give the Symphony Orchestra a repertoire session on his father's Tenth Symphony; and other conductors who worked with this orchestra included Stanislaw Skrowaczewski, then principal conductor of the Hallé.

For the spring opera season Massenet's *Manon* was performed in a joint production with Opera North and was again conducted by David Lloyd-Jones. The producer was Richard Jones, so the College audience was one of the first to witness the 'white box' setting which he and his designer Richard Hudson favour. Manon was sung by Sally Harrison, with Simon Keenlyside as Des Grieux. There were also three performances of Menotti's *The Consul*, conducted by Sian Edwards. In this, Julia Parrott's Magda Sorel and Adèle Paxton's Secretary attracted critical praise. A new name came into the brochure on 7 May when, in the Senior Recital series, a pupil of Barbara Robotham, the soprano Amanda Roocroft, sang in a programme of Purcell and Britten. Simon Keenlyside added to his list of awards in July in the Walter Gruner *Lieder* competition. Bruno Caproni won the second Frederic Cox prize, Claire Daniels won the Miriam Licette Scholarship and the tenor Stephen Rooke won the Sir Anthony Lewis memorial prize.

Two of the College's young composers were successful – Paul Kellett won the Theodore Holland Award and Richard Taylor the Silver Medal of the Worshipful Company of Musicians. (Taylor's *The Journey to Ashanti* was given its first performance by the RNCM Symphony Orchestra, conducted by Timothy Reynish, on 27 June.) Two years' study in Cologne was the cellist Clive Greensmith's reward for being joint winner of the Julius Isserlis Scholarship and a violinist, Michael D'Arcy, won Radio Telefis Eireann's competition for young musicians. And a recent graduate, Claire Moore, took over from Sarah Brightman in London in the leading female role in Andrew Lloyd Webber's *Phantom of the Opera*. Even more spectacular, Ida-Maria Turri, still a student, took over the role of the Countess in Opera North's new production of *Le nozze di Figaro* at the dress rehearsal and sang in all subsequent performances.

The year brought changes. Lord Rhodes died on 14 September. He was Lord Lieutenant of Lancashire when the final decisions on establishing the new college were taken and he had maintained a keen and friendly interest in it. He was intensely musical, played the cornet and founded the Saddleworth Festival. He was known as 'a character' and he was much loved. Among the new members of staff were Stefan Janski (Opera Studies), Ryland Davies and Honor Sheppard (Vocal Studies), and Edward Warren (senior tutor in woodwind). Derrick Wyndham, who had taught piano at the RMCM for almost 20 years, retired from the School of Keyboard Studies. Suffice it to say that his pupils included Anthony Goldstone, Peter Donohoe and Stephen Hough. Wyndham's wife, Sylvia Jacobs, also retired from the School of Vocal Studies. She too had taught at the RMCM. One of her youngest pupils was the star of the *Manon* production, Sally Harrison.

Honorary Fellowship was conferred on the American cello teacher Donald McCall, a former tutor in the School of Strings, Rodney Slatford, Head of the School of Strings, Harry Mortimer, the 'father' of the brass band movement, and the Polish composer Witold Lutoslawski, whose Third Symphony was performed in the evening by the College Symphony Orchestra conducted by Ole Schmidt, who the previous August had been appointed as the orchestra's chief guest conductor. The Honorary Members were Sir Brian Young, then chairman of the Arts Council's music panel, Kenneth Green, director of Manchester Polytechnic, Elaine Bevis, producer of plays for the Opera Studies school and teacher of diction and dialogue, and Frank Mais, the College Secretary.

The honour for Mais was not only an acknowledgment of five difficult years' work but of what was in store in the future. For a new Education Bill had been promised in the Queen's Speech in June and a Government White Paper on higher education had already been published. This gave warning that all polytechnics and selected colleges (which included the RNCM) would be granted corporate status. This meant a new constitution for the College which would sever its links with the four local authorities, abolish the Court and Council and replace them with a Board of Governors. There was to be a Polytechnic and Colleges Funding Council (PCFC) which would expect each polytechnic and college to be active in finding new sources of revenue. Manduell foresaw problems. He realised that the music colleges would confront challenges different from those affecting polytechnics:

> Being essentially monotechnics, we shall have only one commodity in which to trade. The pessimist – or should we say realist? – would expect partnerships with industry, for example, to be more readily capable of realisation by, let us say, the engineering department of a polytechnic than by a bunch of musicians. But the optimist might well counter – dare we say legitimately? – that if we can offer to the nation young people to enrich the lives of our community by their art, then are we not offering them something infinitely more precious and valuable than any consignment of machinery?

Brave words to utter in an essentially philistine country.

Half of Britain's conservatoires were not directly affected by Kenneth Baker's Education Reform Act. The Royal Academy of Music, Royal College of Music and Trinity College of Music were, like the RNCM, to be funded by the PCFC but the London colleges were already corporate bodies. To chart the RNCM's course to incorporation, Sir Denis Forman chaired a 'Formation Committee' which acted in partnership with the College management's steering committee. Even before the Act had been conceived, the RNCM had been generating extra revenue by letting itself out for conferences by such companies as IBM, ICL and Kellogg's. This was intensified; and the catering department also brought in revenue by taking orders for outside events (it supplied, for example, thousands of sandwiches to the Crucible Theatre, Sheffield, for the three weeks of the world snooker championship). The Rambert Dance Company played two seasons a year in the Opera Theatre and box office returns generally were the highest in the College's existence.

Sir Denis Forman, Chairman of the Formation Committee in 1988, with the Duchess of Kent, who conferred Companionship upon him, in 1993. Photograph: Camera Five Four

During 1988 the College's links with foreign conservatoires were extended. In the spring Alain Louvier, director of the Paris Conservatoire, visited the RNCM and agreed to a programme of four study visits. The first took place in November in the Salle Gaveau when string quartets from the Conservatoire and the College jointly performed. Simon Towneley attended the concert. The 12-year exchange programme with Belgrade Academy ended, but an RNCM string quartet participated in Czechoslovakia's celebration of British music and a group of cellists, led by the tutor Moray Welsh, visited Moscow. Joseph Ward's opera students performed Mozart and Menotti in the Isle of Man and various groups from the School of Wind and Percussion visited Holland, the United States, the Channel Islands and the Isle of Man (this became a regular 'date'). And, of course, the RNCM Chamber Orchestra gave 16 concerts in France, including six at the Aix Festival, and took a new work by the Manchester composer Geoffrey Poole.

In the early part of the year the College joined with all other Mancunian music organisations in a month-long festival of music by Debussy and Tippett. Sir Michael, although only just recovered from a major operation, worked infectiously and enthusiastically with the students at the College and at Chetham's as well as with the Hallé, BBC Philharmonic and Manchester Camerata. The College contribution, devised by Christopher Yates, included on 20 January a performance of *A Child of Our Time* conducted by Timothy Reynish. The soloists were Amanda Roocroft, Louise Crane, Andrew Wicks and Deryck Hamon, with the RNCM Chorus and Symphony Orchestra. The composer was moved to tears. His great oratorio was preceded by Debussy's *La damoiselle élue*, with Ida-Maria Turri and Mary Plazas as soloists. A rarity at this festival was extracts from the music of Debussy's uncompleted opera *Rodrigue et Chimène*, presented at the RNCM on 5 February by Richard Langham-Smith.

The spring opera season in March comprised five performances of Verdi's *Rigoletto* and four of Mozart's *Così fan tutte*, the former produced by Stefan Janski and designed by Michael Holt, the latter by Joseph Ward, with designs by Matt English. Both operas were conducted by Noel Davies of ENO, although David Angus conducted one *Rigoletto* performance. In the title-role of the Verdi, Bruno Caproni's success won him a Royal Opera contract, while Geraint Dodd, who sang the Duke, had been 'borrowed' back from WNO, and Sally Harrison, the affecting Gilda, now sings with ENO. Caproni's successor in January 1988 as winner of the Frederic Cox Award, Amanda Roocroft, sang Fiordiligi in the Mozart and moved one critic in *Opera* to write that 'for sheer potential, at this stage in her development' he had not heard her equal.

Sir Michael Tippett (centre right) and Timothy Reynish (left), congratulate Chorus Master Brian Hughes after the performance of A Child of our Time in the 1988 Tippett/ Debussy celebration. Photograph: Lawrence Photographers

Ole Schmidt, Principal Guest Conductor 1987-1990, with the RNCM Symphony Orchestra. Photograph: Lawrence Photographers

Dame Joan Sutherland, who gave a master class during 1988, talks to Amanda Roocroft (centre) and Sally Harrison. Photograph: Lawrence Photographers

The other singers in *Così* included Louise Crane as Dorabella, Stephen Rooke as Ferrando and Deryck Hamon as Guglielmo. These operatic successes were the 'shop window', but they were founded on the work done in David Jordan's Opera Unit in workshop presentations. During 1988 these tackled works by composers ranging from Monteverdi, Gluck and Handel to Tchaikovsky, Puccini, Strauss and Britten.

This was a vintage period for College music-making. Take the concert on 28 April by the College's contemporary music ensemble, Akanthos, directed by another of RNCM's outstanding conducting graduates, Anne Manson, and introduced by Douglas Jarman, in which works by Henze, Ross Edwards, Judith Weir and Schoenberg were performed. Or the master class by the American baritone Sherrill Milnes. Or an evening by guitar students. Or the RNCM Symphony Orchestra's concert conducted by Ole Schmidt which included Nielsen's Fourth Symphony and extracts from *Götterdämmerung* with Jane Eaglen as Brünnhilde. In April the cello tutor Ralph Kirshbaum organised the first international cello festival which brought to the College recitals and master classes involving 15 of the world's best cellists.

Leading musicians continued to visit the RNCM: the percussionist Evelyn Glennie; the fortepianist Melvyn Tan; and Alfred Brendel, who in March waived his fee to give an unforgettable recital of Schubert piano sonatas in aid of an annual prize for the performance of Schubert open to pianists, singers and chamber ensembles in rotation. On 12 and 14 June the German mezzo-soprano Brigitte Fassbaender gave a recital of *Lieder* by Schumann and Wolf and a *Lieder* master class after which the RNCM *Lieder* Prize was awarded to Edith Pritchard. Master classes were also given by Dame Joan Hammond, Dame Joan Sutherland and Richard Bonynge, a notable recognition of the College's operatic eminence.

There was also a delightful 'surprise' concert on 8 March, which was a few days after John Manduell's sixtieth birthday. He was summoned to the Concert Hall at 6pm on the pretext that he was needed to sort out a disagreement there. When he entered, he found an invited audience of friends and colleagues waiting to enjoy a concert in his honour at which music by Schubert, Schumann, Lennox Berkeley, Debussy, Stravinsky, Anthony Gilbert, Abe and Poulenc was performed by Adèle Paxton, Ronan O'Hora, Christopher Underwood and others.

John Manduell would have been less than human if he had not filled his reports at this time with a catalogue of the College's achievements. There was good news of the College's composers and of the Junior Fellows in Conducting – Sian Edwards conducting Tippett at Covent Garden, David Angus chorusmaster at Glyndebourne, Christopher Gayford and David Drummond with staff appointments at Scottish Opera, Gareth Jones ditto at WNO and Anne Manson a staff conductor at Leipzig Opera and working with Mecklenburg Opera. There was also En Shao, holder of a Fellowship established to honour the name of Lord Rhodes, a champion of Sino-British relations. En Shao won the Eduard van Beinum Scholarship organised by Hilversum Radio and he was soon offered a post with the BBC Philharmonic (and later with the Ulster Orchestra).

The 1988 Honorary Fellows reflected some of the year's successes. Ian Kemp, then professor of music at Manchester University, was Tippett's biographer, for example. He received his honour in company with Brendel, Kirshbaum, Sutherland and Bonynge. The College recipients were the senior accompanist John Wilson and the senior tutor in percussion Ian Wright. Honorary Membership was conferred on Professor Stanley Henig and David Hunter. Sidney Palmer, the College bursar, retired and was succeeded by David Kent. The press officer Judy Watt was succeeded by Marian Blaikley; Keith Bond and George Hadjinikos retired from the teaching staff; and through her election as a Manchester city councillor, the College lost one of its favourite catering staff, Irene Summers.

Evelyn Glennie gives a master class.
Photograph: Lawrence Photographers

XII *In the Market Place*

Vesting Day for the reforms under the new Education Act was 1 April 1989. All went smoothly as far as setting up a Board of Governors to replace the Court and Council was concerned. The end of the Council meant the end of Sir Charles Groves's chairmanship. Of all the good friends the RNCM was fortunate to acquire from its inception, Sir Charles was among the best. His resolute determination that standards should not suffer, whatever the economic situation, was the *Leimotif* of all Council meetings. The College did not lose his statesmanship, for he was appointed to the Board, on which he served until his death in 1992. The Board's first chairman was Sir Idwal Pugh, and the College was again fortunate that it found what Lady Thatcher would call 'a believer' in its cause.

But trouble arose over finance. The departure of the four local authorities meant that the College had to replace about a fifth of its revenue income. The Board's first task was to reduce staff by 10 per cent and to make savage cuts in a wide range of activities. The College submitted a strategic plan to the PCFC (the funding body). The Board's main problem in dealing with the PCFC was that the PCFC had little conception of what a music college's needs were. It was flummoxed by a 6:1 teaching ratio and judged everything by the conditions obtaining in polytechnics. Undoubtedly, too, the PCFC expected the transition from one form of College government to another to be effected with unrealistic speed. Also, fewer misleadingly optimistic signals about the amount of grant to be expected would have encouraged the RNCM to embark earlier on some economy measures.

The College was now in the market-place. The Duchess presided in October 1989 at the launch of a drive for partnership between business and the College. Influential businessmen were nominated to the Board, all with strong interests in music. Thus among the new names were Sebastian de Ferranti (chairman of the Hallé Concerts Society), David Hunter (then chairman of Buxton Festival), Christopher Kenyon (chairman of the University Council), and Robert Scott, who organised Manchester's successful bid to be nominated as British contender for hosting the 1996 Olympic Games and steered the launch of the College's business initiative. Also on the Board were the president of the Students' Union and Mrs Elizabeth Smith, assistant manager of the College's Catering Department, who

Sir Idwal Pugh addresses an audience of businessmen at the 1989 launch of a drive for partnership between business and the College. In the background, left to right, Christopher Yates, Robert Scott and the Duchess of Kent. Photograph: Lawrence Photographers

had come to the College in 1980 for seven weeks to help a friend with paper work and had stayed ever since. But for every director of industry or commerce who joined the Board (which first met on 16 December 1988), many more were sought as sponsors and supporters of the College. Heaven and his bathroom scales know how many lunches and dinners Chris Yates ate in furtherance of these objectives.

In the Queen's Birthday Honours List, gazetted in June 1989, John Manduell was knighted. The honour, as readers will have realised by now, was well earned. He had never lost sight of his original aim to put the College at the top and to accept only the best for it. His energy and industry were astonishing. Look at whatever influential committee you liked, J.M.'s name was likely to be there. He had been on the Arts Council's music panel, he was on the board of the Royal Opera, he was chairman of the Composers' Guild, a director of the National Youth Orchestra and a member of several bodies concerned with the music colleges. For 20 years now he had been running the Cheltenham Festival. He was indefatigable and sometimes exasperating. He had colleagues, however, who knew his tendency towards extravagant ideas and would say to him 'Look, John, you just *can't* do that.' And he would at least listen. He persuaded many exceptional people to join the College staff and to work for him for a long time. He could be ruthless and also indulgently soft-hearted. But nothing would interfere with his concern for the students. They were brought up in the College to understand the jungle that awaited them when they began their careers. Nevertheless, when an avaricious agent, in the interval of an opera, went backstage to persuade a talented singer to sign a contract, he was ejected into the street by Manduell and told never to return to the College.

But all this activity took its toll. At Cheltenham in July he was quite seriously ill and spent the festival in a hospital bed. Not long afterwards, he had a heart

Sir John Manduell CBE, Principal of the College, who was knighted in June 1989. Photograph: Hanya Chlala

The first meeting of the new Board of Governors. Left to right: Christopher Yates, County Councillor Peter Nurse, Dr Colin Beeson, Robert Scott, Sir Charles Groves, David Hunter, Sir John Manduell, Sir Idwal Pugh (Chairman), Frank Mais (Clerk in attendance), Lewis Anderson (in attendance), Simon Towneley, Christopher Kenyon, Michael Kennedy, Elizabeth Smith, Daniel Storer (President of the Students' Union), Joyce Hytner. Not present were Sebastian de Ferranti, Professor Stanley Henig and Garth Roberts. Photograph: Petrina Photos

The British Gas North Western jazz improvisation prize.
Photograph: Peter Oldham

Yehudi Menuhin opens the trade fair at the 1989
International Conference of the European String Teachers
Association, with Rodney Slatford, Head of Strings.
Photograph: Lawrence Photographers

attack. It is entirely characteristic that, recognising the symptoms while he was driving alone to London down the M1 and preferring to avoid unknown territory, he drove on for many miles, parked outside the Royal Opera House where he was to have attended a meeting, and asked the commissionaire to park his car and call an ambulance. After a day or two in St Thomas's Hospital, he had various telephones installed wherewith to conduct College and other business until Lady Manduell intervened.

To the annual events in the College such as the Young Musician of the Year and the conference of the Association of Symphonic Bands and Wind Ensembles was added the *Daily Telegraph*'s national 'jazz in education' festival. British Gas offered a prize for jazz improvisation and the College's Big Band, with Clark Rundell directing it with the panache of a latter-day Glenn Miller, was in increasing national demand. Five hundred delegates from throughout Europe attended the international conference of the European String Teachers' Association presided over by Yehudi Menuhin.

As for the College's own music-making, it brought in the usual harvest of prizes. Ian Fountain, at 19, was the youngest winner of the Arthur Rubinstein international piano competition in Tel Aviv. An American postgraduate pianist, Mark Anderson, won the Newport competition and his compatriot Andrea Sokol the Joanna Hodges piano competition in California. Nearer home, in competitions at Brighton and Dudley, College students took first and second prize in each – the pianists Steven Osborne and Jonathan Middleton and Graham Scott and Paul Janes. En Shao won Hungarian TV's international conducting contest and Christopher Gayford took first prize at the Besançon conducting competition.

The operas in March were again ambitious. Richard Vardigans conducted Handel's *Alcina* in a stylishly inventive production by Jamie Hayes, designed by Richard Marks, in which Amanda Roocroft's performance of the title-role again inspired the writer in *Opera* magazine to superlatives: 'In 40 years of listening to young singers, I have never before heard, at this stage in development, a phenomenon to surpass Miss Roocroft … The potential here would seem to be limitless.' Within months of leaving the RNCM, this soprano (who also played the cornet in a Lancashire brass band) was singing leading roles with WNO, Glyndebourne Touring Opera and soon made her début, again in leading roles, at Covent Garden, Glyndebourne, ENO, Paris, Amsterdam and Munich. There were splendid performances in *Alcina*, too, from Sally Harrison as Morgana, Gail Pearson as Oberto and Stephen Rooke as Oronte. Incidentally, the alto section of the chorus was composed entirely of counter-tenors. The second opera was Janáček's *From the House of the Dead*, memorably produced by Stefan Janski and sung (for the first time in England) in Czech – with English surtitles, the RNCM's first use of them. The cast had been taught and coached by Jarmila Hickman. The conductor was Ole Schmidt and the strong cast included Peter Ruane, Andrew Slater, John Daszak and Geoffrey Browne.

Yet, ambitious as these productions were, greater was to come in December when Verdi's *Don Carlo* was staged in the Modena version of 1886, sung in Italian and conducted by Schmidt (Christopher Gayford conducted one performance). The production by Janski, designed by Richard Marks, was extremely handsome, the sets enhanced by costumes borrowed from the Royal Opera's famous Visconti staging. 'Everything looks and feels right,' Andrew Clements wrote in the *Financial Times*, and described this 'glorious evening' as 'an almost unqualified triumph, blazing with conviction and vivid commitment from first to last'. There was fine singing from David Ellis as Posa, Pavlo Hunka as King Philip and Andrew Slater as the Grand Inquisitor. Edith Pritchard was a dignified and melancholy Elisabetta and Sara Fulgoni impressed many critics with her idiosyncratic Eboli – here, one felt, was an exciting new College star in the ascendant. The title-role was sung by Peter Ruane, who succumbed to laryngitis after one and a half acts on the first night, but mimed while Colin McKerracher sang from the pit. The production won the *Manchester Evening News* 1990 Theatre Award for Opera and was recorded on video.

Retirements of two of the original staff of the College occurred in 1989. Terence Greaves had been both Dean of Development and of Undergraduate Studies, acted as Principal in 1984-5 and again during Manduell's illness, and had taken a major creative part in the shaping of new courses. Percy Welton, Head of the School of Academic Studies since 1980, was largely responsible for developing academic courses within the ambience of a college devoted to performance. Another major loss was David Jordan, formerly of the RMCM, who had for 12 years been Director of Opera Studies. The reputation of his department spoke for his achievement and his range of sympathies as a conductor was wide and, perhaps, underrated. Joseph Ward succeeded him, combining the roles of Head of Vocal Studies and of Opera Studies. Shirley Blakey retired as a piano tutor but not as administrator of the successful Junior School (two of its pupils were to reach the finals of the 1990 Young Musician of the Year competition). The Honorary Fellows this year were Sir Harrison Birtwistle, Philip Ledger, Principal of the Royal Scottish Academy of Music and Drama, Peter Graeme, senior oboe

Amanda Roocroft in the title-role of the 1989 production of Handel's Alcina.
Photograph: Gerry Murray

Sara Fulgoni as Eboli in the 1989 production of Verdi's Don Carlo, which won the Manchester Evening News Theatre Award for Opera that year. Photograph: Gerry Murray

Geoffrey Jackson, who succeeded Percy Welton as Head of School of Academic Studies in 1989. Photograph: Lawrence Photographers

tutor since the College opened, Ole Schmidt, Ryszard Bakst and Yossi Zivoni. Honorary Members were Mavis Fox, the orchestra manager, Isobel Ward, a former student who was a worker for the disabled and a victim of multiple sclerosis, and Philip Jones, head of the promotions department.

The RNCM in 1990 welcomed the Earl of Gowrie's report on the three publicly funded London music colleges in which it was suggested that the Royal Academy and the Royal College should merge. This surprising decision was not without self-interest for, as Manduell said in his annual report, 'not unnaturally, we also concluded that if this proposal to provide enhanced funding for a single college in London were adopted, comparable provision should logically follow in an appropriate measure here.' As could have been forecast, the merger plan got nowhere except for amalgamation of the two colleges' opera departments.

Meanwhile the RNCM had made its own changes under the new constitution. Christopher Yates became Vice-Principal, a new office, and Colin Beeson Academic Registrar, another new office taking in much of what had formerly been done by Terence Greaves as Dean of Undergraduate Studies. Lewis Anderson was Administrative Registrar responsible for the very considerable amount of work involved in making the College 'independent' operationally. There was a new Secretary, Colonel George Cauchi, taking over from Frank Mais. An American head of a music college once said of his administrative staff, 'they get on with making it work while we get on with the music.' That is what Vaughan, Mais and Cauchi, the College's three Secretaries, have done *par excellence*.

A new venture, as part of the College's policy to broaden students' horizons, was instituted under the direction of Dr David Ward – music therapy, made possible through grants from Opportunities for the Disabled; and in September the College became the first conservatoire to have a course for brass bands, established under the senior tutor in brass, Howard Snell. Seven students were admitted as first recruits. Another RNCM 'first' was opera sponsorship from Shell (UK) which subsidised Joseph Ward's production in June of Britten's *A Midsummer Night's Dream*, with John Piper's sets and costumes from the Covent Garden production of 1961. Simon Clulow and Barry Deuison shared the role of Oberon and Susan Roper and Maria Tasker that of Tytania. Andrew Slater and Ian Waddington alternated as Bottom and Paul Westhead played Puck at all performances, which were conducted by Christopher Gayford. The second performance, on 24 June, was dedicated to the memory of the beloved soprano Elizabeth Harwood, who had recorded Tytania with Britten. She had died of cancer at the age of 52 on 21 June. An award was created in her memory, the first in 1992 going to Rosalind Sutherland from a panel headed by Dame Janet Baker.

Earlier in the month Michel Brandt had conducted the chamber orchestra in a performance of Poulenc's *La voix humaine*, with Mary Plazas as the woman gradually realising that her lover has deserted her (this was repeated at Aix-en-Provence in June). The College opera performances were part of an Olympic Festival, held to support the first of Manchester's two vain attempts to be chosen as host for the Games. Twenty events were held at the College in June, ranging from Big Band concerts to a photography exhibition. The Manchester bid was acknowledged in the December awards ceremony, when Dr James Grigor, chairman of Manchester Development Corporation and of the Olympic Festival, and Robert Scott, initiator of the bid, were made Honorary Members alongside Lewis Anderson, the Administrative Registrar, and Christopher Gable, artistic director of Northern Ballet (as the Northern Dance Theatre had become known). There was a new and worthy holder of the College's highest honour, Companionship, in Simon Towneley, vice-chairman (until November 1993) of the Board of Governors, chairman of the recently formed Development Committee, and a veteran of the committee which originated and built the College. (He was made a Knight Commander of the Royal Victorian Order in the New Year Honours of 1994 – to the delight of all his friends.) Fellowships were conferred by the Duchess on Trevor Wye, recently retired as principal flute tutor since 1973, and the contralto Alfreda Hodgson, a 'star' former pupil of the Northern School of Music, who in the evening sang Brahms's *Alto Rhapsody* with the Symphony Orchestra conducted by Sir Charles Groves. Alas, she too, like Liz Harwood, was to die of cancer at 52 within two years. At this concert Debussy's *La Damoiselle élue* was repeated, with Sara Fulgoni as one of the soloists.

Among the College's award-winners in 1990 were the Glaswegian soprano Rosalind Sutherland (Frederic Cox prize), Mary Plazas (National Federation of Music Societies/Esso Award), the trumpeter Martin Winter (Leggett Award), Brendan MacBride (Webster Booth Esso Award), Stephen Gadd (Ferrier Memorial Scholarship), Alison Hudson (Ferrier Decca Prize, which had been won by Amanda Roocroft in 1988), the pianists Monika Konopko (Stresa international piano competition) and Graham Scott (Stephania Niekrasz Prize), the baritones Simon Keenlyside (Elly Ameling competition) and Paul Whelan (Fassbaender *Lieder* Award), Gregory Smith (winner of the under-21 category in Paisley organ contest) – and the RNCM Students' Union won the first competition for music colleges' football teams.

The Music Therapy course in progress.
Photograph: Lawrence Photographers

Col. George Cauchi,
Secretary since 1990.
Photograph: Hanya Chlala

XIII *Awesome Testimony*

The Junior Strings Project. Photograph: Chris Thomond

Michael Watson, the resident luthier.
Photograph: Hanya Chlala

There was a point in 1989-90 when the College could have become insolvent. It was a race against time. Before the end of the financial year, the RNCM needed to eliminate the deficit resulting from the cessation of local authority support. This was done, not a little owing to the wise chairmanship of Sir Idwal Pugh and to the College's Vice-Principal, Secretary, Bursar and Administrative Registrar. Government bureaucracy, with all its procedural complications, was spreading the snare-net of red tape whichever way one turned. Signs of the College's new status were now becoming visible. The Concert Hall became the Royal Insurance Concert Hall under a three-year sponsorship agreement. The Recital Room became the Lord Rhodes Room, re-furbished with funds from Seton Healthcare. The bar and refectory were re-designed by Martin Angell and 11 new corporate clients were added to the catering department's list. The annual report listed a page and a half of sponsors and two and a half pages of supporters. Friends of the College who were no longer alive also helped it – the personal libraries of Dame Eva Turner and John Ogdon came into its possession. The Ogdon collection contained much valuable material including scores and working notes of two unpublished operas and the autograph manuscript of his *Kaleidoscope*.

Nor had the appetite for innovations diminished. One during 1991 was the Manchester Junior Strings Project, designed to create chances for children in the neighbourhood of the College to make music by learning stringed instruments and to provide opportunities for string students to acquire specialist techniques in the teaching of young children. Rodney Slatford's pioneering initiative was another example of the College's involvement with the community outside its walls. Penny Stirling directed the project, which was funded by the Leverhulme Trust. A second new venture was the idea of a resident luthier to build a full complement of matching instruments to equip a baroque ensemble. In due course, Michael Watson was appointed.

Newcomers to the staff included three in the School of Keyboard Studies, Arnaldo Cohen, David Sanger and Allan Schiller and three in Academic Studies, Michael Graubart, Josephine Jackson and Stephen Robertson. Among those who retired were Derrick Cantrell and Donald Mearns (Academic), Elizabeth Parry (strings), Catherine Wilson (Vocal), Melvyn Poore, Hugh Potts, Michael Purton, Richard Simpson and Roger Winfield (Wind), and Gillian Weir (Keyboard). All would be missed, but none so much as Robert Elliott, for 13 years Head of the Keyboard School and a teacher at the College from its first day and the RMCM before that. He was succeeded, from 1992, by Renna Kellaway (the School was run in the interim by Christopher Yates). A partial retirement was that of John Bower, who had nevertheless agreed to stay to oversee the work of the recording department which he had created with flair and skill. His successor in 1992 was Barry Ainsworth, with John Egan continuing as assistant.

It was known, too, that Joseph Ward would be resigning as Head of Opera Studies and School of Vocal Studies to pursue a freelance career as a producer. He won the *Manchester Evening News* Opera Award for outstanding services to theatre in Manchester. 'It is mainly due to his guidance and leadership that the College is pre-eminent,' the citation stated. If that leadership had occasionally meant tantrums and high-tension drama, that was only in the tradition of opera and the results he achieved, the singers he set on the right path, testify to his extraordinary ability which, at its best, had the touch of genius. Many stories are told about Joe. On one occasion, after he had reprimanded students for lateness and poor attendance at rehearsals, he arrived next morning at 9.30 for a rehearsal he believed was at 10.00 but in fact was at 10.30. Finding the opera theatre empty, the fire-curtain down, and no sign of stage or music staff, in his fury he decided to set the stage himself. Trying to raise the fire-curtain, he pulled the wrong lever and activated the sprinkler system. Like the sorcerer's apprentice in *Fantasia*, he couldn't stop the water, which flooded the stage. Result: the day's rehearsals had to be cancelled and Joe contemplated resignation (for about 30 seconds).

As it happened, neither of the 1991 operas was Ward's work. In March, Ryland Davies made his début as a producer with an effervescent *L'elisir d'amore* in which Rosalind Sutherland and the Chinese tenor Yu Jixing sang Adina and Nemorino. Yu, wrote Peter Marchbank in *The Guardian*, 'has that Italianate quality which sends shivers down the spine.' The conducting of Christopher Gayford won universal praise. A real donkey was in the cast and, as might have been expected, left its mark in an obvious way. The production was revived in December. Equally stylish was Stefan Janski's production of *The Marriage of Figaro*, memorably well conducted by Timothy Reynish and with a cast of newcomers – Paul Whelan and Maria Tasker as the Almavivas, Anne O'Byrne as Susanna, improving act by act, Michael Pearson as Figaro and a Brazilian mezzo, Laura Santos, as Cherubino. Every seat was sold.

The College's wind orchestra, under Timothy Reynish, made history in July by being the first orchestra from a conservatoire to play at the Henry Wood Proms.

(above) Joseph Ward, Head of Vocal Studies 1986-1991, with the Manchester Evening News Theatre Award given to him in 1991 for services to opera. Photograph: Kenneth Jarvis (middle) Rosalind Sutherland is congratulated by Anne Ziegler on winning the 1991 Webster Booth Esso Award. Photograph: Lawrence Photographers (below) Renna Kellaway, Head of Keyboard Studies since 1992. Photograph: Lawrence Photographers

The RNCM Wind Orchestra outside the Royal Albert Hall on the day of their BBC Promenade Concert, 1991. Photograph: Hanya Chlala

Its programme included works by David Bedford and Nicholas Maw and won plaudits from the critics. Reynish has made the College the national centre of wind-band music. Under his aegis and thanks to his enthusiasm and skill, the RNCM Wind Ensemble and Wind Orchestra have broadcast frequently, made recordings and given the world or British premières of many works, starting with Simon Holt's *Mirrormaze* in 1981 and Martin Butler's *From an Antique Land* in 1982, both commissioned by Sian Edwards when she was a student. Other world premières have included Michael Ball's *Omaggio*, Irwin Bazelon's *Midnight Music*, David Bedford's *Praeludium*, Richard Rodney Bennett's *The Four Seasons* and trumpet concerto, Anthony Gilbert's *Dream Carousels*, Edward Harper's *Double Variations*, Geoffrey King's piano concerto, Nicholas Maw's *American Games*, Geoffrey Poole's *Sailing with Archangels*, Philip Wilby's *Firestar*, *'and I move around the Cross…'*, and *Laudibus in Sanctis*, Colin Matthews's *Toccata meccanica* and Thea Musgrave's *Journey through an Antique Land*. Among the 478 works performed by the RNCM Wind Orchestra between 1978 and 1993 were John Adams's *A Short Ride on a Fast Machine*, Antheil's *Jazz Symphony*, Bennett's *Morning Music*, Bridge's *Pageant of London*, Britten's *Russian Funeral Music*, Michael Colgrass's *Winds of Nagual*, John Corigliano's *Gazebo Dances*, Edward Gregson's tuba concerto, Robin Holloway's *Entrance; Carousing; Embarkation*, Constant Lambert's *Mr Bear Squash you all Flat*, Colin McPhee's *Concerto*, Anthony Milner's *Symphony*, Priaulx Rainier's *Ploermel* (which it recorded), Guy Woolfenden's *Gallimaufry* and Frank Zappa's *The Dog Breath Variations*.

In other fields the College continued to add to its roll of honour. It had a clean sweep in the Ferrier Memorial Scholarship. The first three prizes went to Mary Plazas, Jane Irwin and Gail Pearson, with Miss Irwin, a mezzo, also winning the Ferrier Decca prize. Sara Fulgoni won the Frederic Cox Prize and the Edward Boyle Music Award. The composer Paul Newland was joint winner of the Royal Philharmonic Society prize for his piano trio *Synchroni* and Simon Parkin's Cello Concerto won two prizes – the jury's and the audience's – at Morley College's centenary concerto competition. Later his fiancée, Hannah Roberts, who had earlier won the Jacqueline du Pré memorial award, performed it at the RNCM. Finally, Steven Osborne won the Clara Haskil piano contest at Vévey.

Two very distinguished international musicians headed the Honorary Fellows, Vlado Perlemuter, visiting tutor in keyboard repertoire since 1973 (illness kept him away from the ceremony) and Brigitte Fassbaender, an inspired and inspiring teacher. They were joined by the bassoonist William Waterhouse, Christopher Rowland, director of chamber music, and Michael Gough Matthews, then Director of the Royal College of Music. The Honorary Members were Michael Freegard, at that time director of the Performing Right Society, and Dr John Zochonis, a philanthropist-businessman.

Joseph Ward's farewell to the College came in 1992 when he achieved a long-held ambition to produce Vaughan Williams's neglected opera *The Pilgrim's Progress*. Since its Covent Garden première in 1951, this 'morality', as the composer called it, had been largely written off as undramatic. Ward convincingly proved otherwise in a staging, designed by Michael Holt, which used the whole of the Opera Theatre in a thrilling manner. The opera, which

Richard Whitehouse as the Pilgrim in the 1992 production of Vaughan Williams's The Pilgrim's Progress. Photograph: Gerry Murray

The Duchess of Kent meets members of the cast of Massenet's Cendrillon (1992). Behind the Duchess: Sara Fulgoni and Craig Smith; foreground centre: Marianne Joseph; foreground right: Claire Bradshaw. Photograph: Lawrence Photographers

requires a very large cast and chorus, was conducted by Igor Kennaway in a way that led many to ask why his work was known abroad but not in Britain, and the long role of the Pilgrim was sung with dramatic fervour by Richard Whitehouse. 'For one music college to field 40 accomplished solo singers is an achievement that puts the RNCM way ahead of its London rivals,' Michael White wrote in the *Independent on Sunday*. In *The Times*, David Fallows declared that the performance 'massively vindicated a neglected work, one that should be seen far more widely than just in Manchester.' All the performances (on 5, 8, 25 and 29 March) were attended by Ursula Vaughan Williams. A two-CD recording was issued and the production is preserved on video. In the Birthday Honours in June, Ward was appointed OBE. The other March opera was *Madama Butterfly*, sponsored for all six performances, produced by Stefan Janski and conducted by Noel Davies. There were two casts, in one of which Rosalind Sutherland sang Butterfly, Yu Jixing was Pinkerton (surely the first oriental Pinkerton in operatic history), and Sara Fulgoni sang Suzuki. The Pinkerton of the second cast, Richard Coxon, won the Clonter Opera Prize in March and was soon singing with Scottish Opera, while Miss Sutherland was an ENO Mimi in 1993. After hearing this *Butterfly*, Fallows wrote in *The Times*: 'The two operas together stand as awesome testimony to the present powers of the RNCM'. A third opera was produced in November/December, Massenet's *Cendrillon*, which had not been staged in England since an Opera Viva performance in London in 1966 (it has since had a production from Welsh National Opera in November 1993). Sara Fulgoni sang the title-role, Janski produced, with designs by Richard Marks, and David Lloyd-Jones conducted.

Not only critical plaudits, but tangible awards continued to flow into the College. Hannah Roberts won the Fournier Award; the trombonist Philip Goodwin won the Leggett Award; three string players, Jane Nossek (who was later awarded the Worshipful Company of Musicians' silver medal), Heather Wallington and Rebecca Gilliver won the finals for their instruments – violin, viola, cello – in the Yamaha Music Foundation's European orchestral strings scholarships; Alice Coote, mezzo-soprano, won the Ferrier Decca Prize; Jane Irwin added to her list with the Frederic Cox Prize; Richard Coxon and Kathleen Wilkinson shared the Webster Booth Esso Award; the mezzo Claire Bradshaw won the Anne Ziegler award; and Edith Pritchard won two Glyndebourne awards, the John Christie and the Erich Vietheer memorial prize.

Joseph Ward was succeeded as Head of the School of Vocal Studies by Neil Howlett, a distinguished baritone with ENO and other companies, who had been a tutor at the Guildhall School of Music and Drama. Stefan Janski became Assistant Director of Opera Studies and was later confirmed as Director, and Alec Crowe became Head of Opera Music Staff in succession to Brian Hughes, who remained as chorus master. Hughes's contribution to the success of RNCM operas and choral performances can hardly be exaggerated, for he is by any standard a leader in his field. Another appointment in this school was that of the opera singer Adèle Leigh, whose performances with Covent Garden were much admired in Manchester in the years when the company toured and who later became the operetta toast of Vienna. She became senior tutor in opera stagecraft. Two other notable singers joined the staff, the soprano Teresa Cahill and the baritone John Noble (who had sung Vaughan Williams's Pilgrim to the admiration of the composer, later recorded it with Boult and sang it also at a Northern School of Music concert performance conducted by Maurice Handford in the Free Trade Hall in May 1970), and Bernard Roberts and Martin Roscoe became piano tutors. With the comings, there also were inevitable goings: retirements included those of Rosemary Walton, long-serving répétiteur, and Ryszard Bakst, who had been a piano teacher throughout the College's existence and at the RMCM before that. On 20 June Sir Charles Groves died, 'the most universally loved friend of every musician in the country', as Manduell described him.

The Grosvenor Building replaced the Museum Building as the College's 'overflow' and accommodated the opera department and the Junior Strings Project. Other physical changes occurred in the Concert Hall and the Opera Theatre which were refurbished and re-carpeted from a substantial award by the Foundation for Sports and the Arts. With the nationwide increase in terrorism and violence, strict security measures were introduced including identity cards and doors which opened to the right people only through electronic wizardry. Distinguished musicians continued to visit the College during 1992. The French composer Jean Françaix celebrated his 80th birthday in November as solo pianist with the RNCM Wind Orchestra in a concert of his music and later cut his birthday cake at a party. His *confrère* Gilbert Amy conducted the Symphony Orchestra in a programme including Birtwistle's trumpet concerto *Endless Parade*, with Martin Winter as soloist, and Timothy Reynish conducted thrilling performances of Mahler's Seventh Symphony in the Concert Hall and in Kendal. Brigitte Fassbaender returned for a recital and a master class. Foreign visits also continued, with 20 RNCM string players taking part in Hans Werner Henze's Montepulciano Festival in July. And while statistics make dull reading, it is

Jean Françaix cuts his 80th birthday cake during his 1993 visit. Timothy Reynish looks on with Roberto Carillo and Xanthe Arthurs, who performed in the concert with M. Françaix. Photograph: Lawrence Photographers

Neil Howlett, Head of Vocal Studies since 1992. Photograph: Lawrence Photographers

Dr Colin Beeson, appointed Director of Development in January 1993. Photograph: Hanya Chlala

Backstage after the Gala concert 1992, left to right: Rodney Slatford (Head of Strings), Matt English (Theatre Production Manager), Philip L. Edwards (Lighting Controller), Stefan Janski (Director of Opera Studies since 1993 and producer of the Gala), Timothy Reynish (Head of Wind and Percussion). Photograph: J. Cocks

nevertheless worth mentioning that during the 1991-2 academic year, 91,123 people used the College library and borrowed 35,770 books and scores and played 25,842 records.

The energising spirit of Madeleine Cauchi as Administrative Assistant to the Secretary of the Association of Friends (Christopher Underwood) was the impetus for a fund-raising gala in aid of the development fund announced by the Duchess the previous December. It was held in the Opera Theatre on 30 October 1992 when Amanda Roocroft returned as a soloist and over 250 students took part in an event produced with superfine flair by Stefan Janski. It was followed by a splendid banquet catered by Martin Angell and his staff and served in the Refectory and on both Concourses. It raised £12,000. The guest of honour was Sir Andrew Lloyd Webber, who was so impressed that he promised that the proceeds from the Manchester gala preview of his *The Phantom of the Opera* should go to the College. This pledge was redeemed on 18 October 1993 and raised £20,940.

At the December Congregation of Awards, ceremonial chairs commissioned from a former student, Jonathan Stockton, were used for the first time when the Duchess conferred Honorary Fellowships on Dr Colin Beeson, who a month later was promoted to the new post of Director of Development, the clarinettist Jack Brymer, the composer Petr Eben, the singing teacher Barbara Robotham, and Claude Viala, cellist and Director of the Geneva Conservatory. The new Honorary Members were Sir Idwal Pugh, retiring chairman of the Board of Governors, Charles Beare, the authority on stringed instruments, Major Adam Johnstone, whose 'generosity of spirit and of action towards us' was saluted by Manduell, and Nicholas Payne, administrator of Opera North who had just been appointed Opera Director at Covent Garden.

XIV Building Plans

In November 1992 Dr James Grigor succeeded Sir Idwal Pugh as chairman of the Board of Governors and continued his predecessor's benevolent and witty manner of presiding over meetings. The Board now had to deal with the successor to the PCFC. The new acronym was HEFCE, Higher Education Funding Council for England, and it had an advisory group for conservatoires under the chairmanship of Sir John Tooley. With Colin Beeson in his new post, David Young took over as Academic Registrar on 1 January 1993. The College now had 600 students.

A success that gave much pleasure in the early part of the year was the College's defeat of the Royal Academy of Music 6-0 to win the intercollegiate soccer shield. But off the field, too, prizes were won. The soprano Mary Pope won the Frederic Cox prize, the tuba player Paul Green the Leggett Award. Jane Irwin was the recipient of the Worshipful Company of Musicians' silver medal and also won the Geneva international music competition. The Ferrier Decca Prize was won by Ruth Peel, with Sara Fulgoni second. Amir Katz won first prize and gold medal in the Maria Canals international piano competition in Barcelona and in September won the Robert Casadesus competition in Cleveland, Ohio. Another pianist, Karen Twitchett, won Alfred Brendel's Schubert competition prize, the public being admitted to the performances for the first time. Claire Bradshaw and Riccardo Simonetti respectively were winners of the Webster Booth Esso and Anne Ziegler awards and Miss Bradshaw also won the James Gulliver competition. Paul Whelan, a former postgraduate student, won the *Lieder* Prize in the Cardiff Singer of the World competition. RNCM graduates Sally Beamish, Paul Newland and Simon Holt were three of the first recipients of the Paul Hamlyn awards for composition.

Over the previous year or so, a Japanese Junior Fellow in Conducting, Sachio Fujioka, had conducted the College Symphony Orchestra, including an engagement at the Ludlow Festival in June. He had worked in Japan with Sir

Dr James Grigor (centre), who became Chairman of the Board of Governors in 1992, with Mrs. Grigor and composer and former staff member Thomas Pitfield at the concert in October 1993 to mark the centenary of the foundation of the Royal Manchester College of Music. Photograph: Lawrence Photographers

The performers in the final concert of the 1992 RNCM Manchester International Cello Festival. Seated: Zara Nelsova and Wolfgang Boettcher. Standing, left to right: Anner Bylsma, Steven Doane, Julian Jacobson, Arto Noras, Paul Coker, Maud Tortelier, Philippe Muller, Ralph Kirshbaum (the Festival's Artistic Director), Ian Brown, Boris Pergamenschikov, Mischa Maisky. Photograph: Lawrence Photographers

Charles Groves, on whose recommendation he came to study at the RNCM. In November he had taken over several engagements with the BBC Philharmonic which had become vacant because of Sir Edward Downes's eye ailment. (In January 1994, Fujioka became assistant conductor of the BBC Philharmonic Orchestra.) Fujioka conducted the College orchestra's final concert of 1993 when Antonio Cucchiara, winner of the 1993-4 Sema Concerto Award, performed Sibelius's Violin Concerto. (This annual award for RNCM students is funded by the northern operation of the Sema information technology group.) In the same programme the recent graduate in composition Ian Crew's *Engravings of Loudun* had its first performance. Earlier in the year, the Canadian undergraduate violinist Julie-Anne Derome had played the definitive version of Berg's concerto in the critical edition by Douglas Jarman. Brad Cohen conducted the Symphony Orchestra on that occasion.

An important development at the College since the advent of Christopher Rowland has been the growth of chamber music, to the extent that 56 groups (including 23 string quartets and 22 piano trios) were in 1993 rehearsing regularly. Many of their performances are recorded so that faults can easily be identified and corrected. The College had had an earlier success with the Brodsky Quartet, who had been playing together for four or five years before they began their undergraduate course. Since then it has produced the Sorrel Quartet (resident at York University 1990-3 and then at Liverpool University on a three-year contract) and the Nossek Quartet. The Sorrel became Fellows in Chamber Music at the RNCM 1991-3, giving concerts and helping with the coaching of student groups. The Nossek (Scholars in Chamber Music) work with the junior ensembles. Two long-established international string quartets, the Vermeer and the Franz Schubert, visit the RNCM every year for residences involving concerts and classes. In addition regular coaching is supplied by members of the School of Strings, notably Roger Raphael, Roger Bigley, Rodney Slatford, Ralph Kirshbaum and by the pianist Renna Kellaway. When the best groups have passed through the comprehensive internal concert procedure, they perform for music clubs and chamber-music societies throughout the country and take part in exchange visits with Paris, Prague and Frankfurt.

During 1993 the cello festival, now a biennial event, was emulated by an International Harp Week in March. There was double bass weekend, a day of percussion – 180 percussionists! – and an instrument maker's day. In February the Guildhall School of Music and Drama, the Welsh College of Music and Drama and the Royal Scottish Academy of Music and Drama visited the College

The first International Harp Week, 1993.
Photograph courtesy The Guardian.

with their own drama productions – respectively Ostrovsky's *The Storm*, Shakespeare's *As You Like It* and Brecht's *The Caucasian Chalk Circle*. A few days later, the College again joined with other Mancunian musical organisations to celebrate a living composer, this time Witold Lutoslawski on his 80th birthday during a festival that also featured music of the Scottish composer James MacMillan. Both composers attended the various concerts. On 6 and 7 February the new Hallé conductor, Kent Nagano, conducted the RNCM Symphony Orchestra in the Concert Hall and in Philharmonic Hall, Liverpool, in Mahler's Third Symphony, a gigantic undertaking. The mezzo soloist at the College was Alice Coote, in Liverpool Jane Irwin. Such a performance by a college orchestra would have been unthinkable 25 years earlier. In June the College Wind Orchestra, under Reynish and Rundell, played at the Aldeburgh Festival, giving the British première of Tippett's *Triumph*, which it repeated at the College two days later.

The music of Aldeburgh's Britten had been prominent at the College during June in events anticipating the 80th anniversary of his birth in November 1913. Christopher Gayford conducted five performances of *A Midsummer Night's Dream* in a production by Geoffrey Saunders. Perhaps this came too quickly after Joseph Ward's 1990 production, for although adequately sung and played, it was deemed ordinary by College standards. More successful was Sally Day's production of *The Turn of the Screw*, conducted by Timothy Reynish and Brad Cohen and with Marianne Joseph impressive as the Governess and Michael Bennett and Mary Pope as Quint and Miss Jessel.

The end of the summer term saw Howard Snell relinquish the post of senior tutor in brass (succeeded by Christopher Houlding) and the departure of Josephine Barber, tutor in German and languages co-ordinator since the College opened (Snell remained a member of the staff of the School of Wind and Percussion). Other RNCM (and RMCM) 'veterans' who retired were Una Bradbury, Marjorie Clementi and David Lloyd of the Keyboard School, John Mitchinson, now Head of Singing at the Welsh College of Music and Drama, the flute tutor Roger Rostron, the violist Simon Rowland-Jones, and Moray Welsh, cello tutor since 1973. New members of staff included two recent graduates, the cellist Hannah Roberts and the trumpeter Martin Winter, and Sir Harrison Birtwistle returned as a visiting tutor in composition.

The College marked the centenary of the foundation of the Royal Manchester College of Music by re-creating on 9 October the first (very long and miscellaneous) recital given there. A commemorative booklet about the RMCM's

Witold Lutoslawski talks to Sachio Fujioka who conducted the RNCM Symphony Orchestra in his Concerto for Orchestra during the Lutoslawski Live! Festival, 1993. Photograph: Lawrence Photographers

Kent Nagano talks to the percussionist Scott Mackenzie during rehearsals of Mahler's Third Symphony performed in Manchester and Liverpool in February 1993. Photograph: Hanya Chlala

Marianne Joseph as the Governess in the 1993 production of Britten's The Turn of the Screw. Photograph: Gerry Murray

Rosalind Plowright presents the 1993 winner of the
Frederic Cox Award, Anneliese Chapman, with her prize.
Photograph: Lawrence Photographers

foundation was written for the occasion by Geoffrey Thomason. On 22 October, the Duchess of Kent 'unveiled' the re-naming of the Opera Theatre as The Daily Telegraph Opera Theatre under a sponsorship agreement and attended an inaugural concert at which Steven Osborne played Albeniz and joined the Big Band conducted by Clark Rundell. The second half comprised Act II of *Die Fledermaus*, produced by Adèle Leigh in a manner which made one hope for the whole opera. Four days later there was a remarkable staging by Stefan Janski of Schoenberg's *Erwartung*, designed by Matt English and with Sara Fulgoni as The Woman. Timothy Reynish conducted.

At the 20th Congregation of Awards, Sir Denis Forman became the College's sixth Companion in recognition of a long association and specifically of his work as chairman of the Formation Committee at the time of the change-over to independence. Honorary Fellowships were conferred on Ian Horsbrugh, Principal of the Guildhall School of Music and Drama, Lydia Mordkovich, violin tutor since 1980, the American baritone Sherrill Milnes, and on three RNCM graduates, the composer Simon Holt, the violinist Peter Manning and the pianist Stephen Hough. In the evening the Duchess attended a recital by three students who had recently won international competitions. Jane Irwin sang Mahler's *Lieder eines fahrenden Gesellen*, Steven Osborne played Schubert's G major piano sonata (D.894) and Amir Katz played works by Scriabin, Fauré and Chopin.

In 20 years, Manduell had never, as they say, let the grass grow under his feet. In November, before the Board's annual meeting, he invited the architects concerned to show the Governors the plans for the long-awaited extension on land adjoining the College, where the car park is at present. The go-ahead was approved by the Board for a timetable under which work would start in the summer of 1995 and be completed by December 1996 ready for occupation in April 1997. The development can be financed even if no central funding is provided. The new buildings fulfil the Board's aim of concentrating all tutorial activity on a single site and will contain additional practice and rehearsal rooms – lack of which has been a prime concern of students – and a new library and a theatre rehearsal space which would be used if Manduell's ambition to establish a European Centre for Advanced Opera Studies at the College is fulfilled.

The advent of 1994 brought no sign of diminution in the College students' prizewinning abilities. The cellist Rebecca Gilliver won the Fournier Award and the trumpeter Tracey Redfern the Leggett Award. The soprano Anneliese Chapman, from New Zealand, won the Frederic Cox Award with a recital of songs and arias by Handel, Gounod, Wolf, Janáček and Bush. She had won the

College's Alexander Young Award the previous year and was the Adele in Act II of *Die Fledermaus* at the Daily Telegraph Theatre inauguration. Another New Zealander, the bass Martin Snell, won the £5,000 first prize in the Leslie and Dorothy Blond Award for Operatic Singing, a new competition held at the College but open to singers throughout the country. In February and March 1994, the College participated in another project, devised by the BBC, involving all Manchester's musical organisations. This was 'Northern Lights', a festival of works by composers closely associated with Manchester. Goehr, Birtwistle and Maxwell Davies were strongly represented as were their successors from the RNCM – Simon Holt, Anthony Gilbert and Martin Butler. At the College on 22 February, Maxwell Davies conducted a concert performance of his opera *The Lighthouse*. In the College's subsequent March opera season, Tchaikovsky's rarely performed *The Maid of Orleans* was lavishly staged, with Jane Irwin as Joan of Arc. It was produced by Stefan Janski and conducted by Paul McGrath. As light relief, it was paired with Cimarosa's *Il matrimonio segreto*. Both were sung in the original language with surtitles.

There this chronicle must end, but the College's activities continue unabated. Over 21 years perspectives have subtly changed. In its role as an arts centre the College was able, in its earlier years, to buy in great recitalists to perform there. While this still happens, although less lavishly, the College is now used as an arts resource and as it has progressed towards its coming-of-age, it has looked outwards to the wider musical community. In this context, nothing has been more important than the successful establishment of such events as the symphonic wind band conferences, the brass band conferences, the cello festivals, and the various 'Days' devoted to specific instruments or crafts. In this way many other musicians are invited into the College's orbit and sphere of influence. These pages represent a momentary looking-back, but the RNCM's true role is to look forward. The next five years will be as crucial as the first five. The extension – for which an earlier plan existed before the tenth anniversary – now looks certain to become reality. Inevitably the time will come when there is a new Principal, who will have a hard act to follow. The RNCM has set a cracking pace for 21 years and this has not gone unnoticed in London, where northern success is never really welcomed. All the London music colleges have recently-appointed Principals who have observed what has been achieved in Manchester and will be determined to wrest back supremacy. But if this book proves anything, it is that the Royal Northern College of Music, Manchester, is still best equipped to take the lead and keep it. I do not doubt that it will.

Jane Irwin as Joan of Arc in the 1994 production of Tchaikovsky's The Maid of Orleans. Photograph: Gerry Murray

I – THE JOINT COMMITTEE FOR THE NORTHERN COLLEGE OF MUSIC

The first meeting of the Joint Committee was held at Manchester Town Hall on 27 October, 1966, chaired by Sir Maurice Pariser. The committee was made up of four representatives from the Northern School of Music and four representatives from the Royal Manchester College of Music, together with representatives from four local authorities, Manchester University, the BBC, the Hallé Concerts Society, the Royal Liverpool Philharmonic Society and the Arts Council. Listed below is membership of this committee between 1972 and 1975.

1972/73

Chairman
Dame Kathleen Ollerenshaw DBE

Vice-Chairman
County Councillor Mrs E Muldoon

Members
Sir Leonard Behrens CBE JP
Professor P Cranmer
Mr J Cruft
County Alderman J Ennis JP
Councillor F Firth
Mr R Godlee
Mr S Gray
Mr A Hague JP
County Councillor Mrs C Harrison
Alderman F Hatton JP
County Alderman J Hull CBE
County Councillor H Hunt
County Alderman Mrs E Hyde
Mr M Kennedy
County Councillor Mrs I Lea MBE
Mr W Lockley
County Alderman Mrs K Lowe JP
Mr A Moon
County Alderman H Nevin
Mr J Padmore
Alderman G Pollard
Councillor Mrs S Shaw
Mr C Smart
Councillor M Stewart
Mr D Terry
Mr S Towneley JP
County Alderman H Vernon JP
Dr E Warburton

Clerk to the Joint Committee
Mr P Inman

Treasurer to the Joint Committee
Mr K Bridge

1973/74

Chairman
Dame Kathleen Ollerenshaw DBE

Vice-Chairman
County Councillor Mrs E Muldoon

Members
Sir Leonard Behrens CBE JP
Professor P Cranmer
Mr J Cruft
County Alderman J Ennis JP
Councillor F Firth
Mr R Godlee
Mr S Gray
Mr A Hague JP
County Councillor Mrs C Harrison
Alderman F Hatton JP
County Alderman J Hull CBE
County Councillor H Hunt
County Alderman Mrs E Hyde
Mr M Kennedy
County Councillor Mrs I Lea MBE
Mr W Lockley
County Alderman Mrs K Lowe JP
Mr A Moon
County Alderman H Nevin
Mr J Padmore
Alderman G Pollard
Councillor Mrs T Roth
Councillor Mrs S Shaw
Mr C Smart
Mr D Terry
Mr S Towneley JP
County Alderman H Vernon JP
Dr E Warburton

Clerk to the Joint Committee
Mr P Inman

Treasurer to the Joint Committee
Mr J Hetherington

1974/75

Chairman
Dame Kathleen Ollerenshaw DBE

Vice-Chairman
Councillor E Robinson JP

Members
Sir Leonard Behrens CBE JP
County Councillor I Bishop
Councillor K Eastham
County Councillor J Finn
County Councillor M Fitzherbert-Brockholes JP
Mr R Godlee
Mr A Hague JP
Councillor J Hill
County Councillor R Jacobs
Mr M Kennedy
County Councillor Mrs I Lea MBE
Mr W Lockley
County Councillor A Maynard
Mr A Moon
County Alderman H Nevin
County Councillor W Nuttall
Mr J Padmore
Alderman G Pollard
Councillor Mrs S Shaw
County Councillor S Smith
County Councillor R Spencer MBE
Mr S Towneley JP
County Alderman H Vernon JP

Clerk to the Joint Committee
Mr P Inman

Treasurer to the Joint Committee
Mr J Hetherington

II – MEMBERS OF COURT

1975/76

Chairman
Dame Kathleen Ollerenshaw DBE

Vice-Chairman
Councillor E Robinson JP

Members
Sir Leonard Behrens CBE JP
County Councillor J Finn
County Councillor M Fitzherbert-Brockholes JP
Councillor D Ford
Mr R Godlee
Mr A Hague JP
Councillor J Hill
County Councillor R Jacobs
Mr M Kennedy
County Councillor Mrs I Lea MBE
County Councillor A Maynard
County Councillor W Nuttall
Mr J Padmore
Councillor Mrs S Shaw
County Councillor S Smith
County Councillor R Spencer MBE
Mr S Towneley JP
County Councillor H Vernon JP

Clerk to the Court
Mr P Inman

1976/77

Chairman
Dame Kathleen Ollerenshaw DBE

Vice-Chairman
County Councillor H Vernon JP

Members
Sir Leonard Behrens CBE JP
County Councillor I Bishop
Councillor K Eastham
County Councillor J Finn
County Councillor M Fitzherbert-Brockholes JP
Councillor D Ford
Mr R Godlee
Mr A Hague JP
Councillor J Hill
County Councillor R Jacobs
Mr M Kennedy

County Councillor Mrs I Lea MBE
Mr W Lockley
County Councillor A Maynard
Mr A Moon
County Councillor W Nuttall
Mr J Padmore
Councillor E Robinson JP
Councillor Mrs S Shaw
County Councillor S Smith
County Councillor R Spencer MBE
Mr S Towneley JP

Clerk to the Court
Mr P Inman (until December 1976)
Mr B Hill

1977/78

Chairman
Dame Kathleen Ollerenshaw DBE

Vice-Chairman
County Councillor Mrs I Lea MBE

Members
Sir Leonard Behrens CBE JP
Councillor K Eastham
County Councillor J Finn
County Councillor M Fitzherbert-Brockholes JP
Councillor D Ford
Mr R Godlee
Mr A Hague JP
Councillor J Hill
County Councillor R Jacobs
Mr M Kennedy
Mr W Lockley
County Councillor A Maynard
County Councillor Mrs M Melrose
Mr A Moon
County Councillor Mrs E Moseley OBE
County Councillor Mrs A O'Connell
Councillor E Robinson
Councillor Mrs S Shaw
County Councillor R Spencer MBE
Mr S Towneley JP

Clerk to the Court
Mr B Hill

1978/79

Chairman
Dame Kathleen Ollerenshaw DBE

Vice-Chairman
County Councillor Mrs I Lea MBE

Members
County Councillor Mrs J Cutler
Councillor F Dale
County Councillor Mrs S Dale
Councillor K Eastham
County Councillor J Finn
County Councillor M Fitzherbert-Brockholes JP
Councillor D Ford
Mr R Godlee
Mr A Hague JP
County Councillor R Jacobs
Mr M Kennedy
Mr W P Lockley
County Councillor Mrs M Melrose
Mr A Moon
County Councillor Mrs E Moseley OBE
Councillor K Murray
County Councillor Mrs A O'Connell
Councillor Mrs D Shelmerdine
County Councillor R Spencer MBE
Mr S Towneley JP

Clerk to the Court
Mr B Hill

1979/80

Chairman
Dame Kathleen Ollerenshaw DBE

Vice-Chairman
County Councillor Mrs I Lea MBE

Members
County Councillor Mrs J Cutler
Councillor F Dale
County Councillor Mrs S Dale
Councillor K Eastham
County Councillor J Finn
Councillor D Ford
County Councillor M Fitzherbert-Brockholes JP
Mr R Godlee
Mr A Hague JP

County Councillor R Jacobs
Mr M Kennedy
Mr W Lockley
County Councillor Mrs M Melrose
Mr A Moon
County Councillor Mrs E Moseley OBE
Councillor K Murray
County Councillor Mrs A O'Connell
County Councillor R Spencer MBE
Mr S Towneley JP
Councillor R Wilson

Clerk to the Court
Mr B Hill

1980/81

Chairman
Dame Kathleen Ollerenshaw DBE

Vice-Chairman
County Councillor Mrs I Lea MBE

Members
Councillor R Byrne CBE
County Councillor Mrs M Case
County Councillor Mrs J Cutler
Councillor F Dale
County Councillor Mrs S Dale
County Councillor J Finn
County Councillor M Fitzherbert-Brockholes JP
Councillor D Ford
Mr R Godlee
Mr A Hague JP
County Councillor R Jacobs
Mr M Kennedy
Mr W Lockley
Mr A Moon
County Councillor Mrs E Moseley OBE
Councillor K Murray
County Councillor R Spencer MBE
Mr S Towneley JP
County Councillor Mrs M Ward
Councillor R Wilson

Clerk to the Court
Mr B Hill

1981/82

Chairman
Dame Kathleen Ollerenshaw DBE

Vice-Chairman
County Councillor Mrs I Lea MBE

Members
Councillor R Byrne CBE
County Councillor Mrs M Case
County Councillor Mrs J Cutler
Councillor F Dale
County Councillor Mrs S Dale
County Councillor J Finn
County Councillor M Fitzherbert-Brockholes JP
Councillor D Ford
Mr R Godlee
Mr A Hague JP
County Councillor R Jacobs
Mr M Kennedy OBE
Mr W Lockley
Mr A Moon
County Councillor Mrs E Moseley OBE
Councillor K Murray
County Councillor R Spencer MBE
Mr S Towneley JP
County Councillor Mrs D Ward
Councillor R Wilson

Clerk to the Court
Mr B Hill

1982/83

Chairman
Dame Kathleen Ollerenshaw DBE

Vice-Chairman
County Councillor M Fitzherbert-Brockholes JP

Members
Councillor F Dale
Councillor D Ford
Mr R Godlee
Mr A Hague JP
County Councillor G Hatton
County Councillor Mrs P Hayward
Mr S Henig
County Councillor Mrs S Jones
Mr M Kennedy OBE
Mr W Lockley
County Councillor K Maynard
Mr A Moon
Mr N Morris
Councillor K Murray
Mr D Owen

County Councillor J Prunty
County Councillor R Spencer MBE
Mr S Towneley JP
Councillor R Wilson

Clerk to the Court
Mr B Hill

1983/84

Chairman
Dame Kathleen Ollerenshaw DBE

Vice-Chairman
County Councillor M Fitzherbert-Brockholes JP

Members
County Councillor J Collins OBE JP
County Councillor W Edwards
Councillor J Gilmore
Mr R Godlee
Mr A Hague JP
County Councillor G Hatton
County Councillor Mrs P Hayward
Mr S Henig
Mr M Kennedy OBE
Councillor H Lee
Mr W Lockley
County Councillor K Maynard
Mr A Moon
Mr N Morris
Councillor K Murray
Mr D Owen
County Councillor J Prunty
County Councillor R Spencer MBE
Mr S Towneley JP
Councillor R Wilson

Clerk to the Court
Mr B Hill

1984/85

Chairman
Dame Kathleen Ollerenshaw DBE

Vice-Chairman
County Councillor M Fitzherbert-Brockholes JP

Members
County Councillor J Collins OBE JP
County Councillor W Edwards
Mr R Godlee

Councillor J Gilmore
Mr A Hague JP
County Councillor G Hatton
County Councillor Mrs P Hayward
Mr S Henig
Mr M Kennedy OBE
Councillor H Lee
Mr W Lockley
County Councillor K Maynard
Mr A Moon
Mr N Morris
Councillor K Murray
Mr D Owen
County Councillor J Prunty
County Councillor R Spencer MBE
Mr S Towneley JP
Councillor R Wilson

Clerk to the Court
Mr B Hill

1985/86

Chairman
Dame Kathleen Ollerenshaw DBE

Vice-Chairman
County Councillor M Fitzherbert-Brockholes JP

Members
County Councillor J Collins OBE JP
County Councillor W Edwards
Councillor J Gilmore
Mr R Godlee
Mr A Hague JP
County Councillor G Hatton
County Councillor Mrs P Hayward
Mr S Henig
Mr M Kennedy OBE
Councillor H Lee
Mr W Lockley
County Councillor K Maynard
Mr A Moon
Mr N Morris
Councillor K Murray
Mr D Owen
County Councillor J Prunty JP
County Councillor R Spencer MBE
Mr S Towneley JP

Councillor R Wilson

Clerk to the Court
Mr B Hill

1986/87

Chairman
Professor S Henig

Vice-Chairman
County Councillor P Nurse

Members
County Councillor J Collins OBE JP
County Councillor M Fitzherbert-Brockholes JP
Councillor J Gilmore
Mr R Godlee
Mr A Hague JP
County Councillor G Hatton
Mr M Kennedy OBE
County Councillor D Kingston
Mr W Lockley
Councillor J Morris
Mr A Moon
Councillor J Murray
County Councillor J Prunty JP
County Councillor G Roper
Councillor Mrs S Shaw
Councillor Mrs W Smith
County Councillor R Spencer MBE
Mr S Towneley JP
Councillor R Wilson
County Councillor R Woodhouse

Clerk to the Court
Mr B Hill

1987/88

Chairman
Professor S Henig

Vice-Chairman
County Councillor P Nurse

Members
County Councillor J Collins OBE JP
County Councillor M Fitzherbert-Brockholes JP
Councillor J Gilmore
Mr R Godlee

County Councillor P Grimshaw
Mr A Hague JP
County Councillor D Kingston
Mr M Kennedy OBE
Councillor J Morris
Councillor K Murray
Mr G Parke-Hatton
County Councillor J Prunty JP
County Councillor G Roper
Councillor Mrs S Shaw
Councillor Mrs W Smith
County Councillor R Spencer MBE
Mr S Towneley JP
County Councillor R Woodhouse

Clerk to the Court
Mr B Hill

1988/89

Chairman
Professor S Henig

Vice-Chairman
County Councillor P Nurse

Members
County Councillor J Collins OBE JP
County Councillor M Fitzherbert-Brockholes JP
Councillor J Gilmore
Mr R Godlee
Councillor P Grimshaw
Mr A Hague JP
County Councillor D Kingston
Mr M Kennedy OBE
Mr W Lockley
Mr A Moon
Councillor J Morris
Councillor K Murray
Mr G Parke-Hatton
County Councillor G Roper
Councillor Mrs S Shaw
Councillor Mrs W Smith
County Councillor R Spencer MBE
Mr S Towneley JP
County Councillor R Woodhouse

Clerk to the Court
Mr B Hill

III – MEMBERS OF COUNCIL

1975/76

Chairman
Sir Charles Groves CBE

Vice-Chairman
Mr S Towneley JP

Members
Miss I Carroll OBE
Mr M Darke
Professor B Deane
Mr R Elliott
County Councillor J Finn
County Councillor M Fitzherbert-
Brockholes JP
Councillor D Ford
Sir Denis Forman OBE
Professor A Goehr
Mr R Gonley
Mr A Hague JP
Councillor J Hill
Mr M Kennedy
County Councillor Mrs I Lea MBE
Mr J Manduell
Professor W Mathias
County Councillor A Maynard
Councillor Dame Kathleen
Ollerenshaw DBE
Councillor E Robinson JP
Mr N Robson
Mr B Sarnaker
County Councillor R Spencer MBE
Mr H Totty
Dr E Warburton
Mr F P Welton
Dr J Wray

Clerk to the Council
Air Commodore M Vaughan CBE

1976/77

Chairman
Sir Charles Groves CBE

Vice-Chairman
Mr S Towneley JP

Members
Miss I Carroll OBE
Mr M Darke
Professor B Deane
Mr R Elliott
County Councillor J Finn
County Councillor M Fitzherbert-
Brockholes JP
Sir Denis Forman OBE
Professor A Goehr
Mr R Gonley
Mr A Hague JP
Mr M Kennedy
County Councillor Mrs I Lea MBE
Mr J Manduell
Professor W Mathias
County Councillor A Maynard
Councillor Dame Kathleen
Ollerenshaw DBE
Councillor E Robinson JP
Mr N Robson
Mr B Sarnaker
County Councillor R Spencer MBE
Mr H Totty
Dr E Warburton
Mr F P Welton
Dr J Wray

Clerk to the Council
Air Commodore M Vaughan CBE

1977/78

Chairman
Sir Charles Groves CBE

Vice-Chairman
Mr S Towneley JP

Members
Mr S Briggs
Dr R Bullivant
Mr M Darke
Professor B Deane
Mr R Elliott
County Councillor J Finn
County Councillor M Fitzherbert-
Brockholes JP
Councillor D Ford
Sir Denis Forman OBE
Mr R Gonley
Mr T Greaves
Mr A Hague JP
County Councillor J Hill
Mr M Kennedy
County Councillor Mrs I Lea MBE
Mr J Manduell
Professor W Mathias
County Councillor A Maynard
Councillor Dame Kathleen
Ollerenshaw DBE
Mr A Precious
Councillor E Robinson JP
Mr B Sarnaker
County Councillor R Spencer MBE
Mr F P Welton
Dr J Wray

Clerk to the Council
Air Commodore M Vaughan CBE

1978/79

Chairman
Sir Charles Groves CBE

Vice-Chairman
Mr S Towneley JP

Members
Dr R Bullivant
Mr M Darke
Professor B Deane
Mr R Elliott
County Councillor J Finn
Councillor D Ford
County Councillor M Fitzherbert-
Brockholes JP
Sir Denis Forman OBE
Mr R Gonley
Mr T Greaves
Mr R Griffiths
Mr A Hague JP
Mr M Kennedy
County Councillor Mrs I Lea MBE
Mr J Manduell
Professor W Mathias
County Councillor Mrs E Moseley
OBE
Councillor K Murray
Councillor Dame Kathleen
Ollerenshaw DBE
Mr B Sarnaker
Councillor Mrs D Shelmerdine
Mr W Snape
County Councillor R Spencer MBE
Mr F P Welton
Dr J Wray

Clerk to the Council
Air Commodore M Vaughan CBE

1979/80

Chairman
Sir Charles Groves CBE

Vice-Chairman
Mr S Towneley JP

Members
Professor R Bray
Dr R Bullivant
Mr C Craker
Mr E Cross
Mr J Cruft
Mr M Darke
Professor B Deane
County Councillor J Finn
Councillor D Ford
County Councillor M Fitzherbert-
Brockholes JP
Sir Denis Forman OBE
Mr R Gonley
Mr T Greaves
Mr R Griffiths
Mr A Hague JP
Mr M Kennedy
County Councillor Mrs I Lea MBE
Mr J Manduell
County Councillor Mrs E Moseley
OBE
Councillor K Murray
Councillor Dame Kathleen
Ollerenshaw DBE
Mr W Snape
County Councillor R Spencer MBE
Mr J Ward
Mr F P Welton
Councillor R Wilson
Dr J Wray

Clerk to the Council
Air Commodore M Vaughan CBE

1980/81

Chairman
Sir Charles Groves CBE

Vice-Chairman
Mr S Towneley JP

Members
Professor R Bray
Dr R Bullivant
Dr E Cross
Mr J Cruft
Mr M Darke
Councillor F Dale
Mr R Elliott
Mr D Ellis
County Councillor J Finn
County Councillor M Fitzherbert-
   Brockholes JP
Councillor D Ford
Sir Denis Forman OBE
Mr R Gonley
Mr T Greaves
Mr A Hague JP
Mr P Jones
Professor I Kemp
Mr M Kennedy
County Councillor Mrs I Lea MBE
Mr J Manduell
County Councillor Mrs E Moseley
   OBE
Councillor K Murray
Mr A Shapland
County Councillor R Spencer
Mr J Thackeray
Mr J Ward
Councillor R Wilson
Mr C Yates

Clerk to the Council
Air Commodore M Vaughan CBE

1981/82

Chairman
Sir Charles Groves CBE

Vice-Chairman
Mr S Towneley JP

Members
Professor R Bray
Dr R Bullivant

Mr E Cross
Mr J Cruft
Mr M Darke
Mr R Elliott
Mr D Ellis
County Councillor J Finn
Councillor D Ford
County Councillor M Fitzherbert-
   Brockholes JP
Sir Denis Forman OBE
Mr R Gonley
Mr T Greaves
Mr A Hague JP
Miss J Hamilton
Mr P Jones
Professor I Kemp
Mr M Kennedy OBE
County Councillor Mrs I Lea MBE
Mr J Manduell CBE
County Councillor Mrs E Moseley
   OBE
Councillor K Murray
County Councillor R Spencer MBE
Mr J Thackeray
Mr J Ward
Councillor R Wilson
Mr C Yates

Clerk to the Council
Air Commodore M Vaughan CBE

1982/83

Chairman
Sir Charles Groves CBE

Vice-Chairman
Mr S Towneley JP

Members
Mr S Barker
Dr C Beeson
Mrs S Blakey
Dr R Bullivant
Councillor F Dale
Mr M Darke
Mr R Elliott
Mr D Ellis
Councillor D Ford
County Councillor M Fitzherbert-
   Brockholes JP
Sir Denis Forman OBE
Mr R Gonley

Mr T Greaves
Mr A Hague JP
County Councillor G Hatton
County Councillor Mrs P Hayward
Mr P Hume
Mr P Jones
County Councillor Mrs S Jones
Professor I Kemp
Mr M Kennedy OBE
Mr J Manduell CBE
Councillor K Murray
Miss J Parrott
County Councillor J Prunty
Professor J Rushton
Professor B Smallman
Mrs J Watt
Mr J Ward
Councillor R Wilson
Mr C Yates

Clerk to the Council
Mr F Mais

1983/84

Chairman
Sir Charles Groves CBE

Vice-Chairman
Mr S Towneley JP

Members
Mr S Barker
Dr C Beeson
Dr R Bullivant
Mr T Chatterton
Mr M Darke
County Councillor W Edwards
Mr R Elliott
Mr D Ellis
County Councillor M Fitzherbert-
   Brockholes JP
Sir Denis Forman OBE
Councillor J Gilmore
Mr R Gonley
Mr T Greaves
Mr A Hague JP
County Councillor G Hatton
County Councillor Mrs P Hayward
Professor I Kemp
Mr M Kennedy OBE
Councillor H Lee
Mr C Long

Mr J Manduell CBE
Councillor K Murray
County Councillor J Prunty
Professor J Rushton
Professor B Smallman
Mrs J Watt
Councillor R Wilson
Mr C Yates

Clerk to the Council
Mr F Mais

1984/85

Chairman
Sir Charles Groves CBE

Vice-Chairman
Mr S Towneley JP

Members
Mr S Barker
County Councillor W Edwards
Mr R Elliott
Mr D Ellis
County Councillor M Fitzherbert-
   Brockholes JP
Councillor J Gilmore
Mr R Gonley
Mr T Greaves
Mr A Hague JP
Dr D Hamer
County Councillor G Hatton
County Councillor Mrs P Hayward
Professor I Kemp
Mr M Kennedy OBE
Councillor H Lee
Mr D Lloyd-Jones
Mr C Long
Councillor K Murray
Miss P Paintal
Mr N Powell
County Councillor J Prunty
Professor J Rushton
Professor B Smallman
Mrs J Watt
Councillor R Wilson
Mr C Yates
Dr D Young

Clerk to the Council
Mr F Mais

1985/86

Chairman
Sir Charles Groves CBE

Vice-Chairman
Mr S Towneley JP

Members
Mr S Barker
Dr C Beeson
Dr R Bullivant
Mr M Darke
Mr R Elliott
Mr D Ellis
County Councillor W Edwards
County Councillor M Fitzherbert-
  Brockholes JP
Councillor J Gilmore
Mr R Gonley
Mr T Greaves
Mr A Hague JP
Dr D Hamer
County Councillor G Hatton
County Councillor Mrs P Hayward
Professor I Kemp
Mr M Kennedy OBE
Councillor H Lee KSG
Mr D Lloyd-Jones
Mr C Long
Mr J Manduell CBE
Councillor K Murray
County Councillor P Nurse
Councillor J Prunty JP
Professor J Rushton
Professor B Smallman
Mr D Smith
Mr J Turner
Mrs J Watt
Councillor R Wilson
County Councillor R Woodhouse
Mr C Yates

Clerk to the Council
Mr F Mais

1986/87

Chairman
Sir Charles Groves CBE

Vice-Chairman
Mr S Towneley JP

Members
Mr S Barker
Dr C Beeson
Mr D Ellis
Mr R Gonley
Mr T Greaves
County Councillor M Fitzherbert-
  Brockholes JP
Councillor J Gilmore
Mr A Hague JP
Dr D Hamer
Miss T Holloway
Mr G Jackson
Professor I Kemp
Mr M Kennedy OBE
Mr D Lloyd-Jones
Mr J Manduell CBE
Professor W Mathias
Councillor K Murray
County Councillor P Nurse
County Councillor J Prunty JP
Mr S Rundlett
Professor J Rushton
Councillor Mrs W Smith
County Councillor R Spencer
Mr J Turner
Mrs J Watt
Mr C Underwood
Councillor R Wilson
County Councillor R Woodhouse

Clerk to Council
Mr F Mais

1987/88

Chairman
Sir Charles Groves CBE

Vice-Chairman
Mr S Towneley JP

Members
Mr S Barker
Dr C Beeson
Mr D Ellis
County Councillor M Fitzherbert-
  Brockholes JP
Councillor J Gilmore
Mr R Gonley
Mr T Greaves
Councillor P Grimshaw
Mr A Hague JP
Dr D Hamer
Mr G Jackson
Professor I Kemp
Mr M Kennedy OBE
Mr D Lloyd-Jones
Mr J Manduell CBE
Professor W Mathias
Councillor K Murray
County Councillor P Nurse
County Councillor G Roper
Professor J Rushton
Mrs E Smith
Councillor Mrs W Smith
Mr D Storer
Mr W Thin
Mr J Turner
Mr C Underwood
County Councillor R Woodhouse

Clerk to the Council
Mr F Mais

1988/89

Chairman
Sir Charles Groves CBE

Vice-Chairman
Mr S Towneley JP

Members
Mr S Barker
Dr C Beeson
Mr D Ellis
County Councillor M Fitzherbert-
  Brockholes JP
Mr R Gonley
Mr T Greaves
Councillor P Grimshaw
Mr A Hague JP
County Councillor P Hall
Dr D Hamer
Mr G Jackson
Professor I Kemp
Mr M Kennedy OBE
Mr D Lloyd-Jones
Mr J Manduell CBE
Professor W Mathias
County Councillor P Nurse
Professor J Rushton
Mrs E Smith
Mr D Storer
Mr W Thin
Mr J Turner
Mr C Underwood

Clerk to the Council
Mr F Mais

IV – BOARD OF GOVERNORS

1988/89

Chairman
Sir Idwal Pugh KCB

Deputy Chairman
Mr Simon Towneley JP

Members
Dr Colin Beeson
Mr Sebastian de Ferranti
Sir Charles Groves CBE
Professor Stanley Henig
Mr David Hunter
Mrs Joyce Hytner
Mr Michael Kennedy OBE
Mr Christopher Kenyon
Sir John Manduell CBE
County Councillor Peter Nurse
Mr Garth Roberts
Mr Robert Scott
Mrs Elizabeth Smith
Mr Daniel Storer
Mr Christopher Yates

Clerk to the Board
Mr Francis Mais

1989/90

Chairman
Sir Idwal Pugh KCB

Deputy Chairman
Mr Simon Towneley JP

Members
Dr Colin Beeson
Mr Sebastian de Ferranti
Sir Charles Groves CBE
Professor Stanley Henig
Mr David Hunter MBE
Mrs Joyce Hytner
Mr Michael Kennedy OBE
Mr Christopher Kenyon
Sir John Manduell CBE
County Councillor Peter Nurse
Mr Garth Roberts
Mr Robert Scott
Mrs Elizabeth Smith
Mr Gavin Woods
Mr Christopher Yates

Clerk to the Board
Mr Francis Mais

1990/91

Chairman
Sir Idwal Pugh KCB

Deputy Chairman
Mr Simon Towneley JP

Members
Mr Mark Bates
Mr Sebastian de Ferranti
Sir Charles Groves CBE
Mr Brian Hill CBE
Mr David Hunter MBE
Mrs Joyce Hytner
Mr Michael Kennedy OBE
Mr Christopher Kenyon
Sir John Manduell CBE
Mr Patrick McGuigan
Councillor Kenneth Murray
Sir Mark Richmond
Mr Garth Roberts
Councillor Kevin Rowswell
Mr Robert Scott
Mrs Elizabeth Smith
Mr Robin Stewart
Mr Christopher Yates

Clerk to the Board
Col George Cauchi CBE

1991/92

Chairman
Sir Idwal Pugh KCB

Deputy Chairman
Mr Simon Towneley JP

Members
Mr Robert Buller
Mr Sebastian de Ferranti
Dr James Grigor OBE
Mr Brian Hill CBE
Mr Roy Jobson
Mr Michael Kennedy OBE
Mr Christopher Kenyon
Mr Paul Lee
Sir John Manduell CBE
Mr Patrick McGuigan
Councillor Kenneth Murray
Mr Garth Roberts
Mrs Susan Scott
Mrs Elizabeth Smith
Mr Robin Stewart
Mr Christopher Yates
Mrs Brigid Zochonis

Clerk to the Board
Col George Cauchi CBE

1992/93

Chairman
Dr James Grigor OBE

Deputy Chairman
Mr Simon Towneley JP

Members
Mr Sebastian de Ferranti
Professor Stanley Henig
Mr Brian Hill CBE
Mr Michael Kennedy OBE
Mr Christopher Kenyon
Mr Paul Lee
Sir John Manduell CBE
Mr Garth Roberts
Mrs Susan Scott
Mr Rodney Slatford
Mrs Elizabeth Smith
Mr Robin Stewart
Mr Christopher Yates
Mrs Brigid Zochonis
Mr Dmitri van Zwanenberg

Clerk to the Board
Col George Cauchi CBE

1993/94

Chairman
Dr James Grigor OBE

Deputy Chairman
Mr Robin Stewart

Members
Mr Charles Allen
Mr Sebastian de Ferranti
Sir Ernest Hall OBE
Professor Stanley Henig
Mr Brian Hill CBE
Mr Michael Kennedy OBE
Mr Christopher Kenyon
Mr Paul Lee
Mr Paul Little
Sir John Manduell CBE
Mr Garth Roberts
Mr Rodney Slatford
Mrs Elizabeth Smith
Sir Simon Towneley KCVO
Mr Christopher Yates
Mrs Brigid Zochonis

Clerk to the Board
Col George Cauchi CBE

V – COMPANIONS

1976
The President, Her Royal Highness
    The Duchess of Kent

1978
Dame Kathleen Ollerenshaw DBE

1983
Sir Charles Groves CBE

1986
Miss Ida Carroll OBE

1990
Mr Simon Towneley JP

1993
Sir Denis Forman OBE

VI – FELLOWS

1974
The President, Her Royal Highness
    The Duchess of Kent
Miss Ida Carroll OBE
Mr Philip Cranmer
Mr Terence Greaves
Sir Charles Groves CBE
Sir Anthony Lewis CBE
Mr John Manduell
Dr John Wray

1976
Mrs Sheila Barlow
Dr Kenneth Barritt
Sir Lennox Berkeley CBE
Mr Clifton Helliwell
Mr James Loughran
Miss Dorothy Pilling

1977
Mr Cecil Aronowitz
Mr Philip Jones OBE
Miss Ena Mitchell
Mr Simon Towneley
Sir David Willcocks CBE MC
Mr Alexander Young

1978 (March)
Dame Isobel Baillie DBE
Professor Basil Deane
Sir Geraint Evans CBE
Professor Friedrich Gürtler
Mr David Jordan
Mr Joseph Ward
Mr Percy Welton
1978 (December)
Dame Janet Baker DBE
Lady Barbirolli
Mr Sydney Coulston
Mr Peter Maxwell Davies
Mr Anthony Hodges
Dame Eva Turner DBE
Mr Gilbert Webster

1979
Mrs Shirley Blakey
Mr Myers Foggin CBE

Mr Yehudi Menuhin KBE
Mr Timothy Reynish
Miss Eleanor Warren

1980
M Michel Brandt
Sr Plácido Domingo
Mr Edward Downes
Mr Robert Elliott
Professor Alexander Goehr
Professor Alun Hoddinott
Mr Geoffrey Jackson

1981
Miss Betty Bannerman
Mr Anthony Gilbert
Sir William Glock CBE
Mr Brian Hughes
Mr Michael Kennedy OBE
Dr David Lumsden

1982
Mr John Cameron
Dr Francis Jackson OBE
Mr Terence Nagle
Dr Hans-Dieter Resch
Mr Christopher Yates

1983
Mr Julian Bream OBE
Mr Peter Donohoe
Mr David Ellis
Mr John Rawnsley
Mr John Williams

1984
Miss Caroline Crawshaw
Sir Peter Pears CBE
Sir Michael Tippett OM
Mr Derrick Wyndham

1985
Mr Eli Goren
Mr John Hosier CBE

1986
Dr Douglas Jarman
Mr John McCabe
Mr Patrick McGuigan
Mr John Ogdon

1987
Mr Witold Lutoslawski
Mr Donald McCall
Mr Harry Mortimer CBE
Mr Rodney Slatford

1988
Mr Richard Bonynge CBE
Mr Alfred Brendel
Professor Ian Kemp
Mr Ralph Kirshbaum
Dame Joan Sutherland DBE
Mr John Wilson
Mr Ian Wright

1989
Mr Ryszard Bakst
Sir Harrison Birtwistle
Mr Peter Graeme
Mr Philip Ledger CBE
Mr Ole Schmidt
Mr Yossi Zivoni

1990
Miss Alfreda Hodgson
Mr Trevor Wye

1991
Frau Brigitte Fassbaender
Mr Michael Gough Matthews
M Vlado Perlemuter
Dr Christopher Rowland
Mr William Waterhouse

1992
Dr Colin Beeson
Mr Jack Brymer OBE
Mr Petr Eben
Miss Barbara Robotham
M Claude Viala

1993
Mr Simon Holt
Mr Ian Horsbrugh
Mr Stephen Hough
Mr Peter Manning
Mr Sherrill Milnes
Miss Lydia Mordkovitch

VII – HONORARY MEMBERS

1979
Mr Alfred Alexander
Mr Brian Hill
Dr Samuel Oleesky
Air Commodore Mansel Vaughan CBE

1980
Mr John Bower
Mr John Boyce
The Rt Hon The Lord Boyle of
    Handsworth
Mr John Tomlinson
Mrs Ursula Vaughan Williams

1981
Sir Denis Forman OBE
Professor Sir Bernard Lovell OBE
Mr Keith Murgatroyd
Mr John Vallins

1982
Sir William Downward
Mr Albert Hague
Wing Commander Sidney Palmer OBE
    DFC
The Rt Hon The Lord Rhodes of
    Saddleworth KG DFC

1983
Mr David Andrews
Mr Richard Godlee
Mr Raphael Gonley
Mr Raymond Slater

1984
Mr James Anderton CBE
The Earl of Harewood
Mr Brian Redhead
Miss Helen Trueman

1985
Mr Peter Moores
Mr Clive Smart
Sir John Tooley

1986
Sir John Burgh KCMG CB
Sir George Christie
Mr James Maxwell

1987
Miss Elaine Bevis
Mr Kenneth Green
Mr Francis Mais
Sir Brian Young

1988
Professor Stanley Henig
Mr David Hunter MBE

1989
Mrs Mavis Fox
Mr Philip Jones
Miss Isobel Ward

1990
Mr Lewis Anderson
Mr Christopher Gable
Dr James Grigor OBE
Mr Robert Scott

1991
Mr Michael Freegard
Dr John Zochonis

1992
Mr Charles Beare
Major Adam Johnstone
Mr Nicholas Payne
Sir Idwal Pugh KCB

VIII – SENIOR OFFICERS

Principal (1971-   )
Sir John Manduell CBE, Chevalier des Arts
    et Lettres, HonDMus(Lancaster),
    HonDMus(Manchester), FRAM, FRCM,
    FRNCM, FRSAMD, HonFTCL, HonGSM,
    FBSM, FMP, FWCMD, FRSA

Dean of Development (1973-80)
Terence Greaves MA, BMus(Oxon),
    FRNCM

Dean of Management (1973-76)
Ida Carroll OBE, CRNCM,
    HonMA(Manchester), FNSM, HonGSM

Dean of Studies (1973-80)
John Wray DMus(Oxon), MA, FRNCM,
    FRCO, FTCL

Dean of Postgraduate Studies (1980-1989)
Christopher Yates MA(Cantab), FRNCM

Dean of Undergraduate Studies (1980-89)
Terence Greaves MA, BMus(Oxon),
    FRNCM, FBSM

Vice-Principal (1990-   )
Christopher Yates MA(Cantab), FRNCM

Director of Development (1993-   )
Colin Beeson BA, PhD(Reading), FRNCM

Secretary

(1972-1982)
Air Commodore Mansel Vaughan
    CBE, FBIM, HonRNCM

(1982-90)
Francis Mais MA(Cantab), HonRNCM

(1990-   )
Col George Cauchi CBE, FCIS

IX – HEADS OF SCHOOLS

School of Academic Studies (School of Theory & Humanities 1973-80)
1973-80: John Wray DMus(Oxon), MA,
    FRNCM, FRCO, FTCL
1980-90: Percy Welton MusB (Dublin),
    FRNCM, GNSM, LRAM, ARCM, FRSA
1990- Geoffrey Jackson MusB
    (Manchester), FRNCM, GRSM, ARMCM

School of Composition & Performance
1973- The Principal
[Associate Head (1973-80): Terence
    Greaves MA, BMus(Oxon), FRNCM,
    FBSM]

School of Keyboard Studies
1973-78: Clifton Helliwell FRMCM,
    FRNCM
1978-91: Robert Elliott FRMCM,
    FRNCM, FTCL, LRAM, ARCO
1992-   Renna Kellaway LRSM, ARCM,
    UPLM (Pretoria)

School of Strings
1973-77: Cecil Aronowitz FRCM,
    FRNCM, HonARCM
1977-84: Eleanor Warren MBE, FRNCM,
    FGSM
1984-   Rodney Slatford FRNCM,
    HonRCM

School of Vocal Studies
1973-86: Alexander Young FRNCM
1986-91: Joseph Ward OBE, FRMCM,
    FRNCM, ARMCM
1992-   Neil Howlett MA (Cantab)

School of Wind & Percussion
1975-77: Philip Jones CBE, FRNCM,
    ARCM
1977-   Timothy Reynish MA (Cantab),
    FRNCM, ARCM